God's Kids Celebrate

by Sherilyn Johnson Burgdorf

AUGSBURG FORTRESS

contents

God's Kids Celebrate

Writer: Sherilyn Johnson Burgdorf
Editors: Rebecca Grothe and Virginia Zarth
Designer: Craig Claeys
Illustrator: Becky Radtke

Scripture quotations are from New Revised Standard Version Bible, copyright 1989 Division of Christian Education of the National Council of the Churches of Christ in the United States of America. Used by permission.

ISBN 0-8066-3825-7

Manufactured in U.S.A.

1 2 3 4 5 6 7 8 9 0 1 2 3 4 5 6 7 8 9

introduction

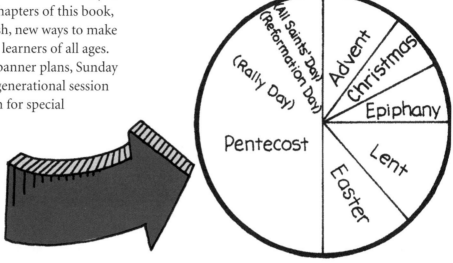

Seasons of the church year

Welcome to God's Kids Celebrate! As you explore the nine chapters of this book, you'll discover fresh, new ways to make the church year come alive for learners of all ages. Activities, bulletin board and banner plans, Sunday school openings, and an intergenerational session work together to help you plan for special celebrations of:

Rally Day
Reformation Day
All Saints' Day
Advent
Christmas
Epiphany
Lent
Easter
Pentecost

The rhythm of the church year includes highs and lows, joyous celebrations and times of penitent reflection. In every Christian's life there are times that match this rhythm: the birth of Christmas and Advent, the growth of Pentecost, the death of Lent, and finally the resurrection of Easter. Helping learners of all ages discover that God is with them through all the seasons of life is at the heart of this book.

In each chapter you will find:

For leaders A section of "Did You Know" facts about the day or season, related Bible readings, and symbols.

Banner A plan for a bulletin board or banner that also will be a learning tool.

Sunday school opening A Sunday school opening worship plan for the day or season that can be used with learners of all ages.

Activity for young learners An age-appropriate activity that makes the season more meaningful to young learners, usually ages 3-7.

Activity for middlers A seasonal activity to spark the interest of older school-age children who can create more independently, usually ages 8-12.

All together now An intergenerational session for the day or season that is designed to engage adults, youth, and children of all ages in learning and growing together. Use "All Together Now" as the basis for special Sunday morning sessions when Sunday school learners invite families, parents, godparents, and grandparents to join them for learning and fun! Or schedule "church nights" once a month when adults, youth, and children can gather for an inexpensive, simple meal followed by an evening of seasonal learning and activity.

Use God's Kids Celebrate as a roadmap to help guide you as you walk the journey of faith throughout the church year. Walk it with prayer, story, activity, and song. And walk it with God's children of all ages!

1

Rally Day

for leaders

did you know...?

To rally can be defined as "to bring to order again" or "to give renewed strength or activity." Rally Day is a joyful time when a congregation rallies its energy behind teaching and learning and renews the baptismal promises of its members to grow in faith.

- Rally Sunday is an ideal time to lift up new projects, themes, or emphases in the church.

- Most congregations celebrate Rally Day on the second Sunday of September.

- The first Sunday school was held in 1780 in Gloucester, England, and was founded by Robert Raikes. For those first Sunday school children, Sunday was their only chance for education since they worked in factories on the other days of the week.

- Rally Day celebrates welcoming, nurturing, education, and faith development. It celebrates a three-way connection among students, their families, and the learning community at church.

- Rally Day is a day for all people and all ages, for those "seasoned" in the church and those who have just arrived: All are welcome!

look it up!

As you prepare for Rally Day, read from the Bible of welcome, learning, and belonging.

Luke 18:15-17
John 15:1-15
Deuteronomy 6:4-9
Luke 2:41-52

symbols of the season

Because Rally Day is not a season of the church year, there is no designated liturgical color for it. However, Rally Day occurs during the season of Pentecost, and the color green used during this season of the church year reminds us that throughout our lives we are called to grow in our Christian faith through education, prayer, and worship.

Bible The Bible brings God's presence to us through the story of Jesus Christ and all of God's faithful people in the Old and New Testaments.

Cross The empty cross is the foundation for all Christian education. Sharing the message of the risen Christ gives purpose and energy to our faith.

Baptismal shell In the promises of Baptism, we have enough to study and practice for our whole lives. The shell symbolizes the waters of Baptism where our faith journey begins: with God's Word and the gift of grace and new life. Rally Day reminds us of the promises given and made at our baptisms.

Balloons and flags The presence of the Holy Spirit gives direction to our Christian education. Flying balloons and other airy and colorful things remind us of the Holy Spirit, ever moving and flowing among us.

a banner for Rally Day

Materials needed: twin size flat sheet in white or a light solid color, 9 sheets of paper, 1 yard of fabric printed in bright colors with a pattern of faces or other festive pattern, bright colors of markers or fabric paint for writing, fusible webbing, scissors, iron.

Rally Day banner

Create patterns for the letters I, A, M, C, H, L, D, F, G, and O from sheets of plain paper. Make each letter about 8" x 10". Use the paper patterns to cut the words "I AM A CHILD OF GOD" out of the printed fabric.

Fuse the letters to the sheet, following the instructions that come with the fusible webbing.

Place the banner on a large table for Rally Day. Invite all learners and teachers who come to Sunday school on Rally Day to write their names on the banner with marker or fabric paint.

Display the banner in the gathering space for your education programs. Throughout the year, invite newcomers to add their names.

Sunday school opening

Preparation: Make a Worship Box by gift-wrapping separately a large box and its removable lid. Put a Bible with a bookmark at Luke 18:15-17 into the Worship Box. Make six 9" x 6" signs out of construction paper. Print one word or letter on each sign: U, R, A, CHILD, OF, GOD. Put a cross on the back of each sign. Place signs in visible spots in the room, but keep letters hidden. (If taping to a wall, have the letter face the wall and the cross be visible.)

As the children enter, greet them warmly. If there are newcomers present, be sure they are sitting by a returning student who can be a friend and guide for the day.

Sing an energetic and festive song that is known by most of the group, perhaps one learned in vacation Bible school.

Introduce yourself and ask for a show of hands for each class or grade. When children see the hands raised for preschool classes, kindergarten, first grade, second grade, and so on, they will realize many different ages are gathered together for learning and worship.

Point out the signs you placed around the room in advance. Ask the children to remain seated and try to spot the signs. Ask for volunteers to bring you the signs.

When all the signs are in front of the group, ask the children to read the letter or word on each sign. Place them on a wall or bulletin board where all can see, but place them out of order. Ask the children to figure out the order of the words/letters to make a sentence. Give the hint, if needed, that the letters U, R, and A can stand alone in place of full words.

Read the sentence together. Then say: **Child of God! That's a very special title. Who is a child?"** (Expect some children to raise their hands.) Bring forward a teen or adult and ask if he or she is a child. Then ask: **"What about me? Am I a child?** (Various answers.) **Who really is a child?"**

Say: **Let's look in the Worship Box to find out. Here's another letter!** (Bring out the Bible.) **The Bible contains many letters from God. They tell us stories about God's people, about God's love and care for us, and especially about Jesus. Here's a story about Jesus and children.**

Read Luke 18:15-17. Say: **That tells me that all of us are to be called children of God, no matter what age we are!**

Pray together, asking the group to echo your phrases: **Dear God, thank you for making us your children. Amen.**

activity for young learners

God's family ID card

Materials needed: fine-tipped markers, clear adhesive paper or laminating sheets, scissors, ink pad.
Preparation: Make two-sided copies of the ID card on Reproducible Sheet 2 on page 50, printing or typing in the name of your church before copying.

Make ID cards for each child to keep in a pocket or backpack as a fun reminder of the link he or she has with your church and with God's family.

Give each child a copy of the ID card made in advance. Have the children draw their own picture in the blank space.

If they are able, have them print their own names, color of their hair, age, and name of your church. Help the youngest children by asking them to dictate information to you or an assistant who will print information on the card for them.

On the back of the card ask children to make one thumbprint above the lettering using the ink pad. Show how they can add a face to the thumbprint using a fine-tipped marker.

When completed, cover both sides of the card with clear adhesive paper or laminating sheets.

activity for middlers

yarn doll

Materials needed: yarn (25 yards for each doll), scissors, hardcover books such as Bibles or hymnbooks, large-eye plastic needles.
Preparation: Make one of the yarn figures.

At the beginning of the year, it is important to build relationships in friendly, nonthreatening ways. Suggest a service project for the students that also gives time to talk as a group about interests and events in the students' lives.

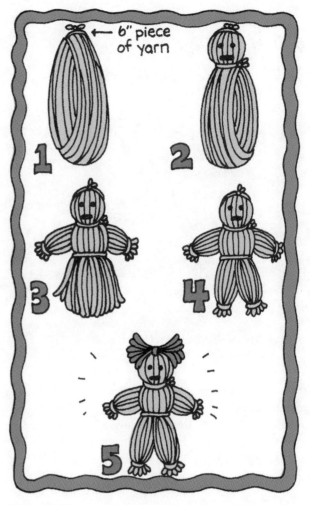

Yarn doll

Say: **Now that Sunday school has started for another year, our church may be welcoming new families to Sunday school and to worship. We can make "God's Kids" quiet toys for young children who come to worship with their families. And the best part is ... the "God's Kids" will be made by you!**

Give each child a Bible or hymnbook. Show the children how to wrap yarn loosely around the book about 70 times. While they are wrapping, read Luke 18:15-17 to them. Talk about the importance of feeling welcome at Sunday school and worship.

1. When there is a thick layer of yarn on the book, slip a 6" piece of yarn under all layers and tie all strands together tightly. Slide the tied loop off.

2. About 1" from the tied part of the loop, tie a 6" piece of yarn to form the figure's head. Add yarn of a contrasting color looped around a few strands on the face of the figure and tied to make eyes and a mouth. Use a plastic needle to thread the ends of those pieces through the figure's head and cut on the other side.

3. Now cut the bottom of the yarn loop and pull one-quarter of the strings of yarn to each side for arms. Tie each arm at the "wrists" and trim the ends of the yarn arms. Tie a piece of yarn around the middle of the doll to make a waist.

4. Leave the yarn below the waist as a skirt for the figure, or separate the yarn in two pieces and tie each one to form legs. Trim the ends of the yarn.

5. Use the same wrapping method to make hair if you choose. Wrap a smaller amount of yarn around a small book, tie it with a 6" piece of yarn, remove from the book and cut the loop opposite the tie. Put a piece of yarn through the figure's "head"; then use it to tie on the hair. Trim the ends.

When the "God's Kids" are finished, they can be presented by the real God's Kids in your group to the worship or hospitality committee as a gift for young children who come to worship. If students wish to keep the God's Kids in the Sunday school room on a bulletin board or take them home, make time to create twin sets—one to keep and one to give away!

all together now
Intergenerational session for Rally Day

welcome!
Materials needed: camera and film, magnifying glass, name tags and markers.
Preparation: In advance, take close-up photos of small, interesting details of objects in and around your church building. At close range, even the most common objects such as the corner of a church pew, a close-up of a portion of the pastor's stole, or a section of a bulletin board may seem new. Have photos developed and ready for this session.

Greet each person individually with a name tag and a warm welcome. Ask returning members to sit with those who are new to the congregation.

Begin the session by singing a familiar and festive song such as "This Is the Day" or a similar one known by all ages. After singing, bring out your magnifying glass.

Say: **Let's take a closer look at this church. Every week there are** (give number) **students of all ages learning about God's promises. On Rally Day we take time to get to know more about our church and our church family. And even though the people in God's family in this place change from year to year, God's love for us never changes. We know that**

God's promises and God's love are waiting for us every day of our lives.

Ask the participants to gather into groups of two or three. Have them look at the pictures and try to identify the object and its location. Ask groups to write down their guesses. Encourage groups to scout the building looking in rooms, the sanctuary, and the narthex to identify any unknown photos.

When all have gathered again, reveal the location and identity of the mystery objects.

Say: **We know that God is with us always— in a classroom or sanctuary, alone or with other Christians, at home or away. We are never a mystery to God!**

explore the story
Materials needed: washable markers.

Read Psalm 139:1-6 for the group. Then teach them hand motions to the verses.

O Lord, you have searched me and known me.
(Cross arms over chest to give self a hug.)
You know when I sit down and when I rise up;
(Arms in front in downward motion, palms down, then back up with palms facing up.)
you discern my thoughts from far away.
(Index finger points to side of head, then points away.)
You search out my path and my lying down,
(Index and middle finger of one hand "walking" on the other arm, held horizontally in front of chest.)
and are acquainted with all my ways.
(Both arms outstretched above head.)
Even before a word is on my tongue, O Lord, you know it completely.
(Index finger points to mouth.)
You hem me in, behind and before, and lay your hand upon me.
(One arm out in front of body, hand turned to make a vertical wall, then the other arm does the same motion; finally both hands meet in the center, one hand on top of the other as if to bless someone.)
Such knowledge is too wonderful for me; it is so high that I cannot attain it.
(Both arms outstretched above head.)

After all have learned the psalm, ask them to use their hands to volunteer to tell their own stories.

Say: **God knows everything about us, but we don't know everything about each other. Rally Day is a time for us to get acquainted by sharing stories.**

Show the learners how to make puppets out of their fists: Make a fist with the thumb tucked inside. With a marker, draw eyes and a nose on the outside of the index finger. Make the puppet talk by moving the thumb up and down.

Divide participants into groups of three or four people, mixing ages. Give questions to the groups, one question every minute or so, and instruct groups to let each person have a chance to answer with their hand puppets. Make questions easy ones to answer such as "Who is in your family?" "What is your favorite thing to do for fun?" "What is your best memory of learning something new?" or "What is your favorite Bible story?" The puppets will help young children feel more at ease and may help those who are self-conscious about talking in a group.

End the sharing time with a large-group prayer.

Pray: **God of all wisdom and love, you know us well and love us always. Be with us in our new year of learning. Help us build a community in Christ as we learn, worship, and pray together. Amen.**

action for all

Come, let us worship

Materials needed: large piece of solid-color fabric, tempera paint (blue, white, purple, green, red), white glue, paintbrushes, wet wipes or a dishpan of warm soapy water.

Preparation: Ask a sewer to hem the edges of the cloth to make a worship altar cloth that will fit the altar or table used during Sunday school opening worship. Mix one part white glue with two parts tempera paint to give paint a more durable finish.

As a way to join all together in the body of Christ, make a worship cloth that can be used during opening worship times in Sunday school. Explain that the colors to be used for handprints are the colors used in worship in the church year, and invite participants to tell which seasons and which colors match. (Blue: Advent. White: Christmas, Epiphany, Baptism of Jesus, Transfiguration, Easter, All Saints' Day. Purple: Lent. Green: season of Epiphany, season of Pentecost. Red: Pentecost Day, Reformation Day, some other special celebrations. For more information about colors, look at the "Symbols of the Season" sections in each chapter of this book.)

Lay the cloth on a large table or two tables pushed together.

Show participants how to use a brush to paint one hand with the tempera paint, then make handprints on the cloth. Be sure all the colors are used. If your group is small, encourage people to make more than one handprint so that there are handprints of all colors all over the cloth.

Make sure there is a place to clean and dry hands before moving to other activities!

Welcome to all!

Materials needed: large sheets of paper, markers.

Mapmaking can be a fun project for all and helpful for those new to your Sunday school.

Divide into smaller groups and assign each group a certain hallway or area of your church building. Ask them to visit the spot and make a map of the area on one of the large sheets of paper. Encourage them to look at the building from a newcomer's perspective: what details would be important to include?

When the groups return with their drawings, tape them together on an empty wall, perhaps one in a well-traveled area close to a doorway.

Remind the group that while they have mapped the church building, they themselves are really the church. The community of Christ is at work wherever its members are—during the week and on Sundays.

A song rally!

Preparation: Ask people of different generations for song suggestions they remember from their Sunday school years.

Spend the final minutes of your time together leading a rally of Sunday school songs, past and present. Begin with songs that would be familiar to all present such as "Jesus Loves Me" or "This Little Light of Mine." Then try a few songs that have been suggested. You may even want to teach a new song to the group that can become the "rallying" song to use each time they meet for an intergenerational event.

2

Reformation Day

for leaders

did you know...?

Reformation Day is October 31, but the church celebrates Reformation Sunday on the last Sunday in October.

- Martin Luther posted 95 theses, statements of Luther's opinions on current church practices, on the door of the castle church in Wittenberg, Germany, on October 31, 1517. He chose this day because he knew that many people would be coming to worship for All Hallow Eve and All Saints' Day. The theses—written in Latin—listed his ideas for re-forming the church of his day, and were an invitation to others at the university to discuss these ideas with him. (This type of posted invitation was a common practice at the university where he taught.) He had not planned for the list to be widely distributed, but someone took it, translated it into German, and printed copies to distribute. This launched a long and great debate with the church in Rome, that led to the formation of Protestant churches.

- In 1667 Reformation Day was pronounced a festival with the "Reformation" name.

- Martin Luther (1483-1546) was a monk, pastor, teacher, musician, father, husband, and theologian. His influence touches our music, our theology, our worship, and our education practices.

look it up!

Read some of the Bible passages that were most influential in the formation of Martin Luther's theology and teaching.

Psalm 46
Romans 3:21-28
John 3:1-21
Ephesians 2:1-10

symbols of the season

The color for Reformation Day is red. The day is a time to refresh our memories of the work of the Holy Spirit, burning within the Christian church. The Spirit is still at work changing and reforming today, just as in Luther's time.

Bible Martin Luther believed it was very important that everyone be able to read so they could study God's Word themselves. The Bible as a symbol reminds us of God's Word, which comes to us through the Scriptures, preaching, teaching, Baptism, Holy Communion, and prayer.

Luther's seal Martin Luther created a seal that includes symbols Luther felt were important understandings about God:

black cross: Jesus' death on the cross for us
red heart: God's great love that gives us life
white rose: trust in Jesus
green leaves: growth in Christ
blue background: a reminder of heaven
gold circle: the never-ending love of God

Luther's seal

Lamp The lamp is used in Scripture to refer to God's word: "Your word is a lamp to my feet and a light to my path" (Psalm 119:105).

a window banner for Reformation Day

Materials needed: scraps of tissue paper (black, red, white, green, blue, and gold or yellow), clear adhesive paper, scissors, craft knife.

Cut an 18" circle of clear adhesive paper. Do not remove the protective paper. On the protective paper covering, draw Luther's seal (see page 51 for a pattern.) Using a craft knife, score the protective paper around each element of the symbol without cutting the adhesive paper.

Cut tissue paper scraps into pieces of various shapes, none larger than ½". The paper used can be different shades of the six colors needed. If this is done as a group project, some participants can be cutting colored pieces of paper as others are placing the mosaic pieces onto the adhesive paper.

Beginning at the outside of the symbol, remove the outer ring of protective paper and place gold or yellow mosaic pieces onto the sticky side of the adhesive paper. There may be a small amount of open space between mosaic pieces.

When the outer ring is fully covered, remove the paper from the blue area and fill it in. Continue toward the center, finishing with the cross.

When the seal is finished, cover it with a second 18" circle of clear adhesive paper. Punch two holes in the upper edge of the circle and string yarn through the holes to make a hanger. Hang the finished seal in a window to appreciate the colorful mosaic work.

Near the window banner, post an explanation of each of the symbols and colors within the seal (see page 9).

Sunday school opening

Preparation: In the Worship Box place items that fit together as pairs such as a right and left shoe, pen and paper, candle and a match. (See page 5 for instructions for making a Worship Box.) You'll also need a recording of the hymn, "A Mighty Fortress Is Our God" or someone to play it on the piano, and a picture of Martin Luther. Optional: Find an "actor" to play the part of Martin Luther, dressing the part and talking about his life.

As the children gather, play the hymn "A Mighty Fortress Is Our God." If the children are familiar with the words, ask them to sing along.

Say: **The man who wrote that hymn lived about 500 years ago in Germany. His name was Martin Luther, and this is what he looked like.** (Show picture of Luther. You may need to clear up any confusion children have between Martin Luther and Martin Luther King Jr., since both were noted religious leaders and reformers.)

Say: **Martin Luther was a pastor and a teacher. He had a wife and children. But the thing that makes him most important to us 500 years later is the fact that he started the debates that led to the formation of Protestant churches, including the Lutheran church, named for him.**

Martin Luther feared for many years that he had done too many wrong things during his life and that God would punish him because he had not followed God's law. But after reading his Bible and studying for a long time, Luther realized that God gives us laws to obey, but also promises us forgiveness, love, and salvation.

Explain to the children that many things in life need to be "paired" with other things to be most helpful. Show the items from the Worship Box as examples. A right shoe is more helpful when the left one is also found. A candle and a match are useful *together*.

Say: **Luther realized that God is just like a parent who loves us very much. God gives us laws, or commands, that will keep order and give guidelines for our lives. God gave us these laws: to love God, love other people, and care for the world. Those are the things we need to do as God's children.**

God also gives us promises. God's promise was sent in Jesus who lived in the world to show us how to obey God's laws, to die on the cross so that we can be forgiven for our sins, and to be raised from the dead to give us the promise of life with God forever, even when we die.

Martin Luther taught that we need both the law and the gospel (promises) to live as God's children. He helped us understand Christian faith and life in a new way.

Pray together the following prayer, based on Psalm 46. Explain the words *refuge* and *exalted* if necessary. Direct the group to grow louder with each repetition, but to say the last one quietly.

Leader: "Be still," God says.
All: **God is our refuge and strength.**
Leader: "Know that I am God," God says.
All: **God is our refuge and strength.**
Leader: "I am exalted among the nations,"
    God says.
All: **God is our refuge and strength.**
Leader: **We need never be afraid.**
All: **God is our refuge and strength.**
Leader: **God is with us always.**
All: **God is our refuge and strength.**

activity for young learners

reforming clay

Materials needed: Play clay (see recipe below); forming tools such as rolling pins, chopsticks, plastic knives, and so on; small zip-closure plastic bags.
Preparation: Make play clay for the children to use: Mix 1 cup flour, 1 cup water, ½ cup salt, 1 teaspoon cooking oil, and ½ teaspoon cream of tartar in a cooking pan. Cook and continue to stir over medium heat until it forms a ball. Let it cool until kneadable, then work it on a floured surface until smooth. Separate dough into smaller portions and add food coloring. Store in airtight containers. This recipe makes clay for five children.

Projects of young children are rarely finished. Their artwork is always "in progress." Use that creativity to help understand the ever-changing image of the church.

Say: **Martin Luther was called a reformer of the church. He saw things happening that didn't seem right to him, so he made changes. And people are still making changes to the church today, reforming the way things are done to make the church a better messenger of God's word to the world.**

If there are readers in the group, print the word "reformation" on a board or on paper. Help them find the word "form" in the middle of the word.

Say: **We can have fun today being "formers" and "reformers." Make something with your clay, then change it or add to it to "re-form" it.**

Give the children the clay and equipment and let them use their creativity to make works of art.

There's no need to expect children to make a finished creation. Send a small amount of the play clay home in a zip-closure bag with each child.

Say: **Use your play clay at home, forming and reforming as much as you wish; and remember Martin Luther, the church re-former!**

activity for middlers

"Your Word" window hanging

Materials needed: dark construction paper, tissue paper, white writing paper, old crayons (yellows, reds, oranges), grater, wax paper, iron, scissors, newspaper.
Preparation: Ask another adult to visit the class and supervise the hot iron. Make an enlargement of the lamp symbol on page 49. Make a sample of the project.

Luther believed that every person should be able to read and study the Bible, so he translated it from Latin, the language of the church of his day, into German, the language of the people where he lived. He wanted the Bible to be the guide for life.

Read together Psalm 119:105. You may want to teach the song "Thy Word" to the group.

Make a symbol picture depicting that verse. Show the students the lamp you made, as an example of a light source with a flame. Tell them to think about a burning, moving flame as a light source and a symbol of the Holy Spirit's presence.

To make the project:

Draw an outline of a lamp on a sheet of dark paper, then cut and remove the lamp shape leaving the background uncut. Also cut a flame hole in the appropriate place on the paper.

"Your Word" window hanging

Choose a color of tissue paper, cut a little larger than the lamp outline, and tape it to the back side of the background paper.

Shave pieces of crayons with a grater onto a piece of waxed paper large enough to cover the flame hole for the lamp. Then cover the shavings with another small piece of waxed paper. Place under some newspaper and carefully press with a warm, dry iron to melt the shavings.

When the crayon has cooled, tape that piece behind the flame cutout on the background paper.

Have the students print Psalm 119:105 on a small piece of white paper and glue it to their finished artwork. Encourage them to display the project in a window so the flame will glow.

all together now
Intergenerational session for Reformation Day

welcome!

Materials needed: white paper, pencils, and crayons.

Greet participants and ask them to join together in pairs, a child with an adult if possible.

Give each pair one piece of paper and ask the youngest of the two people to draw a random design on the paper.

After the youngest artist is finished, the other person in the team takes over and "reforms" the design into a recognizable picture.

Switch roles, having the oldest artist draw a random design on the back of the sheet, then the younger to fill in details that he or she thinks are missing.

Compliment the artists on their ability to change the drawings into something new, on their "re-forming" skills.

Say: **Today we will celebrate Reformation Day, a day when we celebrate the beginning of Protestant churches, including the Lutheran church. We'll learn about the man for whom the church is named, Martin Luther, and think about the reforming of God's people going on today.**

explore the story

Preparation: Make a list of 10-12 scavenger hunt items that would be accessible in and around your church building and that have some significance to Luther's story. Include items such as a Bible; a worship book or hymnal with a hymn by Martin Luther in it; a rubbing from the foundation of the church building; a catechism; a baptismal towel or candle and a communion glass (symbols of Baptism and Communion); and possibly even a person with a German background!

Divide participants into teams, four or five people on each team.

Say: **Martin Luther wanted everyone to be able to read the Bible, so he translated it from Latin, the language of the church at that time, into German, the language spoken by the people where Luther lived. He wanted everyone to understand the mass, or worship service, better. So he created the "German mass," a worship service that was spoken and sung in German, understood by all.**

We can usually understand the words spoken to us, but can we always remember and do them? Let's try a "Hear and do" scavenger hunt—no pencils or paper allowed!

Read the list of items to the group. Read slowly and repeat the list two or three times. Give them explanations of what the items represent in the life story of Martin Luther. Tell the group you will stay in the room to give reminders if they forget part of their list.

Send the groups out to look for the needed items. When they have returned, ask them to look up one of the Bible passages listed in the Reformation Day "Look it up!" section on page 9. Read the passage together. Then use hymnals to sing a hymn by Martin Luther such as "A Mighty Fortress Is Our God," "God's Word Is Our Great Heritage," or "From Heaven Above."

action for all

Family of Faith Flags

Materials needed: large sheets of light-colored construction paper; crayons and markers; fabric scraps, beads, and other miscellaneous craft items; scissors; glue.

Preparation: Bring in a picture of Luther's seal (see the version on page 51), or point out the window banner described on page 10 if you made one.

Say: **Martin Luther was a reformer of the church. He reformed key church teachings and practices, he reformed worship, he reformed how children and adults were taught about God, and he reformed people's ideas about themselves and** about God. **This symbol helps us understand some of the beliefs Luther felt were central to our Christian faith.**

Explain the symbols in the seal.

Divide participants into groups of four or five. Give each group a large piece of paper and ask participants to create their own "family of faith flag." Encourage them to use drawings, words, or symbols on the flag to represent the people and mission of your congregation. (Or, families may choose to make a flag representing their family.) The flag itself may be a significant shape, such as the shape of a book for readers or teachers, a globe to represent mission, a clef sign for musicians.

Display the family of faith flags along with the Luther seal on a clothesline hung in a fellowship hall or other well-traveled area.

Saints and Sinners

Materials needed: balloons or sponge ball, a net or string.

Preparation: Use the net or piece of string as a divider hung about 5 feet above the floor to create a volleyball-style court.

Martin Luther was often in conflict with himself. As a young man he knew he was a sinner, so he felt he needed to be punished for his sins. He tried to make up for his sinful actions by fasting and studying and praying. But he never felt good enough. Finally he realized that we are all "saints and sinners" at the same time. God loves us! God gives us forgiveness and new life in Baptism. But we are still sinners. No matter how hard we try, we can't erase our own sins.

Groups may be able to better understand the "saint and sinner" concept by playing a volleyball-style game.

To begin playing "Saints and Sinners," all players start on the same side of the divider. Play begins when a balloon is tossed up in the air. After a person bounces the balloon into the air, he or she moves quickly to the other side of the net or divider. The balloon, however, stays on the original side and is tossed back and forth between players still on that side.

When only one person is left on a side, he or she tosses the balloon across the net, then goes under the net to join the other players. While he or she is moving, someone else begins the balloon toss,

moving back to the original side again. Play continues between the "saint and sinner" sides as long as you wish.

When the game is finished, families can talk together about daily examples of what it means to be a saint and a sinner. Ask: **How does God's great gift of forgiveness shape the way we live each day?** (We can act in confidence to serve God and other people. When we sin or fall short of "saintly" actions, we know God is ready to hear our confession and to forgive us, giving us a fresh start each day.)

Table Talk

Materials needed: devotional books or magazines, calendar.

Martin Luther wanted every family to talk about Christian life at home, so he wrote two catechisms, one especially for home use. And as a teacher, Luther often had students at home with him during mealtime for "table talks," informal conversations about faith.

Distribute family devotional books or magazines to each table or each family. There are excellent books as well as magazines published quarterly for young and old alike. Encourage families or groups at tables to turn to the devotion for the day and have their own "table talk" for a few minutes to close the session today.

Optional: Since Advent is still weeks away, ask small groups to participate in making a book of "Table Talks" for the Advent and Christmas season. Each group can sign up to write one day's story, draw some artwork, or share thoughts about a scripture passage. Stories can then be collected at a later date and printed in a booklet to be given to all members of the congregation and friends for their own Table Talks during the Advent/Christmas season.

3

All Saints' Day

for leaders

did you know...?

All Saints' Day is celebrated on November 1. The first Sunday of November is traditionally observed as All Saints' Sunday.

ⓖ All Saints' Day follows "All Hallow Eve," (All Saints' Eve) known as Halloween (October 31).

ⓖ All Saints' Day is a time to remember Christian witnesses, or saints, living and dead, who have sought to faithfully live out their baptisms. Many churches include the names of their members who have died during the past year in their worship bulletins and prayers on All Saints' Sunday.

ⓖ The custom of remembering all martyrs of the church on one specific day has been done since the third century.

ⓖ Some of God's saints are commemorated on their own days during the year and others are honored on "lesser festivals." (See page 52 or look in a worship resource book for a listing of saints.)

look it up!

Read these texts about God's faithful ones, some of which you may hear in worship on All Saints' Day.

Revelation 7:9-17
Revelation 21:1-8
Ephesians 1:11-23
Matthew 5:1-12
Hebrews 12:1-2

symbols of the season

White is the color for All Saints' Day. One of the hymns associated with All Saints' Day—"For All the Saints"—refers to the host of saints standing before God in bright array. Newly baptized Christians are dressed in the white robe of righteousness (Galatians 3:27) and often at funerals the coffin is covered also covered with a white pall (cloth). The symbolism of white stays with us as we journey from birth through death.

Heavenly city, new Jerusalem The symbol of a new city, a new heaven, and a new earth come from Revelation 21 and are the final destination for all of us as God's saints.

A regal throne This symbol recalls the image from Revelation 7 of God reigning at the end of time from a glorious throne, with a great multitude of saints from all nations and all time standing before the throne.

Christ, the Lamb John 1:29 and John 1:36 refer to Jesus as the Lamb of God. This image is also used in Revelation, especially Revelation 21:22-27 and Revelation 22:1-5, to identify Christ as the Lamb at the final coming, surrounded by the saints.

Body of Christ All of God's people, living saints and those who have died, are joined as the body of Christ.

Alpha and omega These two Greek letters that are the beginning and the end of the Greek alphabet signify the beginning and the end of time. "I am the Alpha and the Omega," says the Lord God (Revelation 1:8; Revelation 22:13).

a banner for All Saints' Day

Materials needed: royal blue fabric, plain paper for patterns, fusible white interfacing for letters and figures, felt or other fabric in colors of many skin tones, an iron, gold fabric paint, scissors.

Use a blue background for the banner to suggest the heavens.

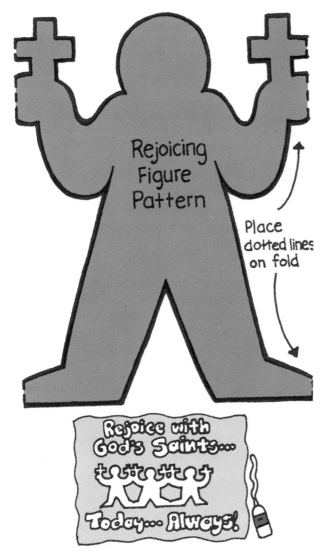

Rejoicing Figure Pattern

Place dotted lines on fold

Rejoice with God's Saints... Today... Always!

"Rejoice with God's Saints" banner

From plain paper folded in accordion folds, cut a pattern for the rejoicing figures, following the illustrated diagram. Enlarge the pattern provided if you like. Cut rejoicing figures from fusible white interfacing to place on the banner. Cut heads for the figures from tans, browns, and ambers to represent the many skin tones of God's saints. Cut letters for the phrase "Rejoice with God's Saints... Today... Always."

Use an iron to attach the white figures, heads, and letters to the backing. Outline the edges of the white fabric pieces with the gold fabric paint. Let dry before hanging.

This could be created as a bulletin board instead of a banner. Invite learners to cut out chains of the rejoicing figures and outline them with gold glitter glue.

Sunday school opening

Preparation: With a crayon, draw a fairly thick cross on a large hand mirror. Place the mirror in the Worship Box. (See page 5 if you need instructions for making a Worship Box.) Refer to page 52 to find information about some saints.

Welcome the children into the room by asking them to sing "When the Saints Go Marching In" with you. Then ask the children what they know about saints. Some may think they are people who have died or who are famous or "perfect." Say: **Today is All Saints' Day. We celebrate today that there are people who have lived their lives as God's people. They are baptized. They strive to follow God's word. Some would say they "walk in God's path."**

Tell children about a few of the saints who would be of interest to them, including men and women. Ask: **Are all saints dead?** (No!) **There are still many people who walk in God's path today. They are saints, too, and are good models for all of us to follow. You probably even know some.**

Say: **Today I have a picture of a whole group of people who are living saints. Would you like to see it?**

Bring out the mirror and turn it so that the children can see themselves in the mirror. Draw attention to the cross on the mirror that marks their image.

Say: **You are saints too! During your lifetime, someone probably said or will say to you, "Child of God, you have been sealed by the Holy Spirit and marked with the cross of Christ forever." When are those words spoken?** (During a baptism).

Explain that Baptism is when we become a saint and join with all of God's saints who have gone before us as workers in God's family.

Pray together: **Dear God, be with your saints today as we walk in your path. Help us reflect your love to all those we meet as we learn, and play, and work. Amen.**

activity for young learners

All Saints' cards

Materials needed: tissue paper in bright colors cut into a variety of 2"-3" shapes, plain white paper or index cards, shallow pans, water, iron, paper towels.

All Saints' card

and shapes remind us of the variety of saints in God's family. No two saints are alike!

Fold the finished sheets in half to make a note card. Have the children make a drawing or dictate a note on the card for a saint they know.

activity for middlers

Saints Signature book

Materials needed: blue tempera paint, dishwashing liquid, straws, water, container with tight-fitting lid, white construction paper, pie pan, stapler, white writing paper, markers.

Preparation: Make the paint mixture by combining 2 tablespoons tempera paint, 1 cup water, and 1 tablespoon dishwashing liquid in a container with a secure lid. Cut white writing paper in 8½" x 5½" pieces.

Read Hebrews 12:1-2 with the students. Ask students to help you name some who would be part of the great cloud of witnesses, great saints such as the disciples, Mary, Martin Luther, Mother Teresa, and leaders from your own congregation.

Say: **Saints aren't all famous people. Look to your right and left: those people are saints, and you are too!**

To make Saints Signature books:

Shake the paint mixture in the sealed container, then pour into the pie pan. With plastic straws students can blow into the mixture and make

Preparation: Locate a drying place for the finished cards where they can lie flat to dry. Make a sample card.

Saints come in all sizes, all ages, all colors. Saints are those who walk in the light of Christ. Children can know they are saints, too.

Say: **At your baptism you become a part of a big family, God's family. When we celebrate All Saints' Day, we remember the people who are in that family. Some are people around you, some lived many years ago. Your own family may have told you the stories of some of them. They are all called God's saints. We live as God's saints, too. We can share Jesus' story and his love with others. Today we will make All Saints' cards to send to a saint you know.**

Give each child a piece of white paper.

Place the cut pieces of tissue paper in a central spot on the table and invite the children to choose the sizes and colors they wish.

Show them how to dip each piece, one at a time, into the shallow pan of water, then slide it along the edge of the pan to remove some of the water.

Place each tissue piece on the white paper. When pieces are arranged to cover most of the paper, lay the sheet aside to dry, tissue paper pieces in place. Use a dry iron to speed drying time and make colors more vivid. (Place dry paper towels above and below the paper before ironing.)

When dry, remove the tissue paper, and the card will be beautifully colored. Tell children the colors

Paint blowing for Saints Signature book

bubbles. Remind the students of the "great cloud of witnesses" as the bubbles begin to rise!

Ask a second person to hold construction paper close to the bubbles, letting bubbles pop onto the paper. Bubbles also can be scooped onto the paper and bubbles will pop as the paper dries, leaving interesting patterns.

When the paper is dry, fold it in half and slip a few of the 8½" x 5½" sheets of paper between the folded bubble sheet, book style. Staple ¾" in from the folded side. Use markers to title the books "Signatures of Saints."

Give the young saints opportunity to collect signatures from each other, then go out into the church building to look for more saints of all ages!

all together now
Intergenerational session for All Saints' Day

welcome!

Materials needed: paper plates (10" diameter for adults, 7" for children), scissors, ¼" elastic (found in sewing and craft departments), markers.

Preparation: Make a saint visor of your own.

Wearing your own saint visor, welcome the "saints" as they arrive. Direct them to the visor-making supplies and invite them to cut and make their own visor.

To make visors:

Cut a paper plate in half (Use a large plate for adults and a small one for children.) Cut a gentle curve on the straight side of the cut and punch a hole in each corner.

Cut a piece of elastic about 10" long. String the ends through the holes punched in the paper plate and tie them to the visor.

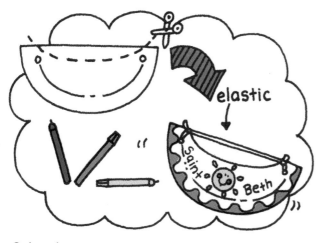

Saint visor

Be creative as you decorate the visor with markers. Print your own name on the visor, including the title "Saint" before your name.

Encourage everyone to wear their saint visors throughout today's session.

explore the story

Materials needed: roll of paper at least 24" wide and 48 feet long, markers, masking tape.

Preparation: Cut paper into 24" sections. Make a copy of page 52 from this book and cut the cards apart.

Gather at tables and sing a song about the saints, perhaps "For All the Saints," "Blessed Are They," or a lively one such as "When the Saints Go Marching In"!

Divide the participants into small groups. Say: **All Saints' Day is a time to celebrate our part in the body of Christ and to celebrate the lives of those faithful Christians who have died. We are all saints of the church. Looking at all of us in our visors, anyone can see that we are called saints. The path walked by saints is not always an easy one. Not everyone is willing to listen to God's word and to strive to live in God's ways. Not everyone is willing to take to heart the promises of Baptism.**

Read Matthew 5:1-12.

Say: **In Hebrews 12:1-2 the saints are called a "great cloud of witnesses." Some churches have pictures or names of these saints in stained glass or other art around the sanctuary. Today you will do a Saints Search using clues. When you have discovered the name of the saint, make a great cloud from the large sheets of paper and print the saint's name on the cloud. Also, print your names on the cloud. You are saints, too.**

Give each group a card made in advance from page 52 of this book. Encourage them to use the Bible passage, if given, to figure out which saint they have.

When the group is able to identify their saint, they cut a cloud-shaped piece from the roll of paper, and then print the saint's name and their own names on the cloud. They may also wish to add names of their ancestors in the faith. As time allows, have groups work on additional cards until all are used.

Tape all of the clouds around the walls of the room, to be surrounded by the "cloud of witnesses."

Give each team opportunity to share information about their saint with the whole group.

Pray this prayer for All Saints' Day:

Almighty God, whose people are knit together in one holy Church, the body of Christ our Lord: Grant us grace to follow your blessed saints in lives of faith and commitment, and to know the inexpressible joys you have prepared for those who love you; through your Son, Jesus Christ our Lord, who lives and reigns with you and the Holy Spirit, one God, now and forever. Amen.

Copyright © 1978 Lutheran Book of Worship.

action for all

Stained-glass saint symbols

Materials needed: black construction paper, tissue paper, transparent tape, scissors, pencils.
Preparation: Find a book that illustrates symbols for various saints. Check with your pastor, church library, or worship planners.

Making a simplified stained-glass design will let each participant take a saint symbol home.

Ask participants to think of a symbol they would like to make into "stained glass." Give possibilities of universal symbols such as a cross, baptismal shell, or others listed above in "Symbols of the Season." Show the reference books of individual saint's symbols. Suggest that some people may be able to find a saint who bears their name and use that symbol. Or participants can create an original saint's symbol.

Draw the symbol on a sheet of black construction paper. Leave wide black strips between sections of the drawing to resemble the lead outlines in real stained glass. Cut out each section carefully without cutting the separating strips in the design.

Lay a second piece of black paper under the cut design and trace and cut out matching holes in that sheet.

Place tissue paper pieces in the open areas of the design and fasten them with transparent tape to the black outline strips.

Glue the two black sheets together with the colored tissue pieces between them.

Add a string for hanging and encourage participants to hang their stained-glass saint design in a window at home.

Envelope bookmarks

Materials needed: used envelopes in any color that have at least two blank corners, pinking shears or other decorative scissors, markers.

A simple bookmark can be an enjoyable gift that can make daily Bible readings or a new book about one of God's present-day saints even more fun to read.

Give each person an envelope of any size or color.

Each person is to cut two corners off an envelope for bookmarks, one to keep and one to give to a friend or family member. For each bookmark, cut across the envelope 2" to 3" from the corner to make a triangle. Use pinking shears or decorative scissors with patterned edges on the blades. Use markers to give bookmarks a special touch.

When the bookmarks are finished, they can be given as gifts to other saints in your congregation or neighborhood, to an adult Bible study group, to homebound saints, or to those who are soon to affirm their baptism at confirmation.

Called by name

Materials needed: paper, pencils and markers.

At our baptism we are called by name to be saints in God's kingdom. What difference does that make in our lives? What should we saints be doing for others? for God?

Ask each person to print his or her first name vertically down the left side of a sheet of paper.

Using each letter in the name, each person will list an action she would like to do, or a trait he would like to have, as one of God's saints. For example:

J   Joyful
O   Offers kindness to newcomers
D   Dedicated to prayer each day
Y   Yearly travels to service camp

Encourage those at tables together to help each other think of saintly traits and actions to list.

4

Advent

for leaders

did you know...?

Advent means "coming" and is a time of waiting for God to act in miraculous ways.

- We recognize three advents or comings: Jesus' birth 2,000 years ago, Jesus' presence with us today, and Jesus' return at the end of time.
- The season of Advent always begins four Sundays prior to Christmas Day.
- During Advent, some countries retell legends of God's servants. They are reminders of the obedience to God's calling that Mary also showed.
- St. Lucia Day (December 13) is celebrated in Sweden and honors Santa Lucia, a girl who according to legend brought food to people during a great famine. On St. Lucia Day, some families are treated to breakfast brought by the oldest daughter, who portrays Lucia.
- St. Nicholas Day (December 6) honors a fourth-century bishop, Nicholas, who is said to have helped the poor by secretly giving them his own earnings. Today, many people celebrate the day by giving gifts secretly.

look it up!

Read some of the familiar texts of Advent in the Bible:

John 1:19-23
Luke 1:26-38
Luke 1:39-80
Isaiah 11:1-10
Philippians 1:3-11

symbols of the season

The color of Advent is blue, for hope and devotion. Mary is often pictured in blue as she waits obediently and faithfully for the birth of God's Son, Jesus.

Advent wreath The most well-known of Advent symbols, the wreath holds four candles for the four weeks of Advent. Gradually the light begins to shine from the darkness, one candle added each Sunday until Christmas comes. The wreath is often a circle of greens, another reminder of the never-ending circle of God's love that surrounds us.

Jesse tree The Jesse tree gives a visual image for the lineage of Jesus written in Matthew 1 and Luke 3. The Jesse tree bears symbols of Jesus' family tree beginning with God's creation of Adam and Eve. It is a wonderful way to tell the story of many biblical characters. It also reflects the prophecy in Isaiah 11:1, "A shoot shall come out from the stump of Jesse, and a branch shall grow out of his roots."

Trumpets The fanfare of trumpets sounds to prepare us for something grand: the entrance of a very important person or the beginning of a grand celebration. The trumpets of Advent prepare us for Jesus' first coming and the final advent when "the trumpet will sound, and the dead will be raised" (1 Corinthians 15:52).

Candles and light Jesus Christ is the light shining in the darkness. The Gospel of John (John 1:1-9) gives us the words of Advent, words that prepare us for a Son that outshines the sun, a light that would enlighten everyone.

Road or path In Isaiah 40:3-5 and Luke 3:3-6 we read "Prepare the way of the Lord, make his paths straight." These words suggest the symbol of a road or path that is made ready for the King, Jesus.

Bulletin board

a bulletin board for Advent

Materials needed: monthly pages from a calendar for the current year, construction paper, paper fastener, poster board, tempera paint, scissors.

As a background for the bulletin board, cover the board with calendar pages. Cut out letters for, or write out the words, "Come, Lord Jesus, be our guest. Let our Advent days be blessed."

Using the Christ Clock on page 53 as a pattern, make a larger version out of poster board. Use paint or markers to color each section with the appropriate church year color. Add a clock hand of appropriate size made from poster board using a long brass paper fastener.

Optional: If space is available to leave the bulletin board up for the rest of the year, move the hand to each appropriate season and create a new heading for the bulletin board for the change of seasons, such as "Jesus has come to us!" (Christmas) or "Season of Stars" (Epiphany).

Sunday school opening

Preparation: Place a timer in the Worship Box. Set it so that it will go off during the opening worship time.

Greet the children and ask them to be seated. Say: **Waiting in line is not easy. And waiting for your birthday is hard, too. Is it hard to wait to open presents or to celebrate Christmas with** your family? (Acknowledge responses.) **Even though waiting can be hard, we usually find we are happy when the time finally comes to open the present or have the celebration, don't we?**

Think of other things that are worth the wait. Write ideas children give on a chalkboard or poster board. Give examples such as baking a cake, waiting for a new baby brother or sister, waiting for spring flowers to bloom, learning to play an instrument, and so on. Bring out the timer. It may give the children more waiting ideas.

Say: **Today we are in the church year season called Advent. During Advent we count down the days until Christmas, just like we're counting down the minutes on this timer. In our Advent songs we sing words like "Wake, awake!" "Prepare...," "Oh, come, oh, come..." Those are words to get us ready for something AWESOME after the wait is over.**

Teach the following song to the children, using the tune for "Jesus Loves Me, This I Know."

Come, Lord Jesus, come to us.
Make your light shine over us.
Help us wait and watch for you.
Through the day and night time, too.

Refrain:
Come! We are waiting. Come! We are waiting.
Come! We are waiting through all our Advent days.

Say: **During Advent we will hear the story of Mary, the mother of Jesus. She was very surprised to hear an angel tell her that she would be the mother of Jesus! But she willingly said, "Here I am." She would wait and listen for God's plan.**

We are waiting during Advent for a much bigger event than a cake or even our own birthdays. We are waiting for Jesus to come!

activity for young learners

clothespin candles

Materials needed: spring-type clothespins, construction paper that is the same color as your church's Advent candles, yellow construction paper, glue; optional—artificial evergreen roping, about 24" per child.

Preparation: For each learner, cut four strips of construction paper ½" x 3½". Use colors that are similar to the ones you use for your church's Advent wreath. Have four spring-type clothespins for each child.

Candles on the Advent wreath are a welcome addition to the dark nights of the Advent season. And candles on evergreens are a tradition said to have been started by Martin Luther in Germany more than 500 years ago.

Young children can make paper candles to place on an evergreen Advent wreath and later on the Christmas tree. The candles will be safe for children to use without the fire concerns of real candles.

Give each child four spring-type clothespins. Have the children glue construction paper strips onto one side of each clothespin.

Clothespin candles

If children are able, let them cut out four flames from yellow construction paper. Younger children may be able to tear a flame shape or may need help cutting.

Place a small amount of glue on the inside of the paper strip at the end that is not the clip and glue the paper flame onto the candle at that point. The candles are now ready for each child's own Advent wreath.

Optional: Give each child a piece of artificial evergreen roping and let them bend the wire into a circle and join the ends together to make a wreath. At home, the candles can be added to the wreath one week at a time.

Say: **When Christmas finally comes, you can put away your Advent wreath and move the candles to the Christmas tree!**

activity for middlers

Christ clock

Materials needed: poster board, brass paper fasteners, scissors, colored pencils in colors that match the church year seasons.

Preparation: Make copies of page 53, enlarging it on your photocopier if possible. Using poster board, cut out patterns for symbols (see pages 49 and 50 for symbol patterns) that will fit in the appropriate sections of the Christ clock for each of the church year seasons: Advent, Christmas, Epiphany, Lent, Easter, Pentecost.

"Wait!" "Hurry!" "We'll be late!" "Is it time yet?" School-aged children understand clock time well. They need to be on a schedule for a good part of their day. Help them understand the cyclical pattern of the church year by making "Christ clocks."

Read Ecclesiastes 3:1-8 to the group.

Say: **The church year is divided into seasons, too. Each season tells us about a portion of Jesus' life.**

Give each student a copy of page 53, the "Christ clock." Cut out the clocks and clock hands.

Talk about the symbols of the church year that were prepared in advance. Explain why each one fits with its corresponding church year season.

Have each student place a symbol under their paper, beneath the season to which it belongs. Use colored pencils that match the church year season colors and do a rubbing of each symbol in the appropriate section of the clock.

Remind students that to use the symbols for rubbings they will need to cooperate, and wait! Use the time to talk with them about the waiting we do in Advent. Ask them what they do at home to wait and prepare for Jesus' coming at Christmas.

Attach a clock hand to the clock in the center with a brass paper fastener to finish the "Christ clock." To make sturdier clocks, mount the completed clock face and hands on poster board before assembling.

all together now
Intergenerational session for Advent

welcome!

Materials needed: 4 sheets of chart paper, markers or crayons.
Preparation: Tape the chart paper together to make a long strip. Secure the paper to a wall.

As you greet everyone coming in for today's event, ask them to think about what they do at home to prepare for the coming of Christmas.

Ask participants to work in small groups to draw outlines of a house or an apartment with a big picture window. In the window draw people preparing in some way for Christmas. Each group adds another residence to the long drawing paper to make a neighborhood scene stretching along the wall.

Talk about ways to prepare for Jesus' coming not only at church, but also at home.

explore the story

Materials needed: books or videos about some of God's messengers, for example: John; St. Francis of Assisi; Lucia; Nicholas, bishop of Myra.
Preparation: Prepare centers where groups can look at the books or videos about the messengers. Optional: In advance, ask people to act out the parts of the messengers highlighted below. Instruct them to learn about their character and come in costume to tell about themselves, such as how they helped tell and show others about God's love.

Say: **During Advent we await the birth of Jesus. For many centuries there have been people who have, by their actions, pointed others to Christ.**

Encourage groups to explore the books, short video segments, or listen to the "guests" that describe the messengers of God's love.

John the Baptist is the most obvious messenger. We read about his birth in Luke 1:8-25,57-80 and his ministry in Mark 1:1-8.

St. Francis of Assisi is another who spent his life helping peasants, lowly and humble, like Mary and Joseph. St. Francis made the gospel speak to the people who needed hope and good news. There is not a festive day set aside for St. Francis during Advent, but the crèche is associated with him.

Lucia was a young Sicilian girl who lived her life helping the poor, giving them food and money. Her name comes from a word meaning "light." After her death, a legend about her spread to Sweden, where St. Lucia Day is an important event celebrated each December 13.

Nicholas of Myra was a bishop in the fourth century. His care for the poor led to the well-known traditions of St. Nicholas who secretly left gifts and other good things for people. Secret gift-giving is still practiced on December 6 in many countries in remembrance of him.

Give families opportunity to talk about others they know who are messengers of God's gospel.

action for all

Pointer painted wreath

Materials needed: green, blue, and yellow tempera paint, white 9" x 12" construction paper, evergreen sprigs, pie pans or shallow paint dishes, scissors, wipes or soapy water, glue, scraps of bright colors of construction paper.
Preparation: Cut fresh evergreen boughs into small 3"-4" sections. If necessary, locate painting shirts or other protective clothing for use while painting.

Say: **People such as John the Baptist, St. Lucia, and St. Nicholas are not the only ones to point the way to Christ by their actions. We can do it, too!**

Ask all to hold up their pointer finger as a candle. Don't forget to light the candles with imaginary flames! Sing "This Little Light of Mine" and include other verses such as "Gonna shine this light around the world, I'm gonna let it shine!"

Say: **The candles on your Advent wreath at home can be a simple way to shine your light for others. When people see the Advent wreath, they will know that you are preparing and waiting for Jesus' birthday at Christmas. We can make Advent wreaths using fingerprints as candles.**

Pointer painted wreath

Give each group or individual a piece of white construction paper. For an interesting way to paint the advent wreath, use a sprig of evergreen. Dip the evergreen in green tempera and take turns rubbing the needles across the paper or simply dabbing the paint on the white paper using only the tips of the needles.

While the wreath is drying, use blue tempera (or the colors chosen for advent candles at your church) and have each group make four pointer finger "candles" on white construction paper for the wreath. Add a yellow paint thumbprint flame to each candle, allow them to dry, then cut them out. Have wipes or soapy water ready for cleaning paint from fingers.

When the background wreath is dry, ask groups to cut four slits in the wreath for candles. Slip the four candles in the four slots and tape the candles in place on the back.

Tack the candles to the front of the picture with small drops of glue. Leave the tops unglued, and fold down the candle flames. As each successive Advent week arrives, a new flame can be unfolded so it "burns."

Add decorative corners of colored paper and the heading "Let it shine!"

Behold! Surprise messages

Materials needed: white paper, white crayons, water-color paints, brushes.

Say: **Imagine what a surprise Mary had when the angel Gabriel came to visit her! Do you remember Gabriel's message to Mary?** (She would be Jesus' mother.) **Using your white crayon and paper, draw a message or picture for Advent.** (You may want to offer some suggestions, such as the words "Jesus is coming!" "Prepare the way of the Lord!" "Wait and trust in God." Pictures might be a candle, an Advent wreath, trumpets, a dawning sun.) **When someone else adds paint to the picture, they'll get an Advent surprise message...from you!**

Give each group or individual a piece of paper and a white crayon. When they have completed their pictures, place them in a pile, then hand them out again randomly so that each person gets someone else's Advent design. Bring out the paints and let everyone reveal their surprise messages by brushing watercolor paint across the entire page.

Say: **Now that you have received a surprise message, find out who created that message for you. Remember them in your Advent prayers.**

A shining sun

Materials needed: white or yellow paper plates, scissors, markers, glitter, glue.

Read Isaiah 60:1-3 to the group. Sing an Advent hymn such as "The King Shall Come" or "My Lord, What a Morning!"

Say: **During Advent many of our Bible readings and hymns mention a new day when Christ will come. We know that on that day Jesus, the Son of God, will outshine the sun that shines each day. Make a bright sun for Advent to place on a light switch at home. Each time you turn on the lights, remember the Son who comes for us all.**

Give each group or individual a paper plate. With scissors, cut towards the center of the plate, stopping about 2" from the center. Continue to make similar cuts every 2" or so going around the plate, leaving the center uncut.

Make a slit in the center of the plate, then cut a hole for a light switch. (1" x ½" is standard size.)

Color the sun with yellows, reds, and oranges.

Print the words "Arise! Shine!" on the center of the sun. Add glue and glitter to make it sparkle.

5

Christmas

for leaders

did you know...?

Emmanuel, also spelled Immanuel, is the name prophesied in Isaiah 7:14 and given to Jesus by the angel in Matthew 1:23. It means "God is with us."

🕭 The season of Christmas is more than just a day. Christmas lasts from December 25 through January 5, the 12 days of Christmas.

🕭 The Hispanic tradition of "Las Posadas" creates a bridge from the last days of Advent into Christmas. It culminates with a party on Christmas Eve that welcomes the "travelers," reminiscent of Mary and Joseph finally finding a place in the stable at Bethlehem.

🕭 Pope Julius selected December 25 as the official date for Christmas Day in the late third or early fourth century.

🕭 In some cultures, people do not start decorating the Christmas tree until December 24.

🕭 St. Francis saw a connection between the refugee conditions of Mary, Joseph, and Jesus and the peasant people of his time. Out of that came the simple setting in the stable that we have adopted into the Christmas story.

look it up!

Read the story of Jesus' birth in the Bible.
Luke 2:1-20
Matthew 1:18-2:12

symbols of the season

White is used as the color for the entire season of Christmas. Even though the commercial culture uses red and green as the colors for Christmas, white is symbolic of the holiness and light of the newborn Christ. It is the color used for all festivals that celebrate the major events in Jesus' life.

Manger and crown The tiny baby Jesus, asleep in a manger, is also seen as king (Matthew 2:1-2). The rugged manger combined with a royal crown is a symbol fitting only for Jesus, true God and true man.

Angel Good news of great joy! The angels are the bearers of news to the shepherds (Luke 2:8-15). They are the first "evangels," or bringers of good news. Angels can be our reminders to share the news, too.

Evergreen tree The symbol of an evergreen tree is a reminder of the eternal, never-failing love from God.

a bulletin board for Christmas

Materials needed: red or white paper to cover bulletin board, Christmas wrapping paper, one large sheet of poster board, large gift bow, construction paper, markers.

Cover the bulletin board with red or white paper. As a caption use the phrase "A child is born..." at the top or bottom of the board, leaving the center open for a "package."

To make the package, fold a large sheet of poster board in half to make a rectangular "present." Cover the outside of the poster board with gift wrap and place the gift bow in the center of one of the folded sides.

With the fold at the top, on the inside of the gift-wrapped "box" print the phrase, "...and he is named Jesus!" Place the finished "gift box" on the center of the bulletin board.

Cut various sized pieces of colored construction paper into gift shapes that will contrast with the

"A child is born" bulletin board

background. On each piece print names given to Jesus, for example, Wonderful Counselor, Son of God, Emmanuel, Christ, the Lord, Savior, and so on. Use various lettering styles, some elegant, some simple.

This bulletin board could be easily adapted to an appliqué banner by using fusible webbing and a printed fabric for the gift and bow in the center. The phrase "...and he is named Jesus!" could be written below the gift box. Use various colors of fabric paint for the headings and the names of Jesus.

Sunday school opening

Preparation: Locate at least two or three different styles of Christmas crèches, including ones that are safe for small hands to touch. Display them at eye level for children and keep the figures of baby Jesus hidden in the Worship Box until it's time to tell the Christmas story. (If you need to make a Worship Box, see page 5 for instructions.)

As the children gather, give them an opportunity to come and look closely at the crèches you have displayed. If the pieces are not fragile, invite the children to pick them up as they wish. Some children may notice that baby Jesus is not yet in the scene.

Ask the children to sit down and listen to the Christmas story.

Say: **Sometimes we call this a manger scene, but it also has another name, a crèche. Long ago in Italy a man named Francis of Assisi decided to make a scene with real people playing the parts of Mary, Joseph, baby Jesus, and all the shepherds, animals, and kings. He wanted the ordinary people of his time to know that Jesus came to earth not in a fancy palace or church, but in a very simple place-- a stable. Jesus came for all people, not just for some.**

Tell the Christmas story from Luke 2:1-20, holding up the individual figures from one of the crèches as the story is told. Stop your storytelling after Mary and Joseph have come to the stable and ask the children to tell you what happens next. (Jesus is born!)

Bring out the Worship Box. Open it to find all of the baby Jesus figures from the crèches. Place them in the mangers.

Teach the children a simple fingerplay by asking them to do the actions as you say the verse. After repeating the verse again a few times, ask them to join you in saying the words to the verse.

Here Is the Stable

Here is the stable *(Form roof's peak with hands.)*
where Jesus was born *(Rock imaginary baby in arms.)*
and was laid in the manger that first Christmas
    morn. *(Motion with cupped hands toward floor.)*
And Mary and Joseph *(Motion to left for Mary, to
    right for Joseph.)*
and cattle and sheep *(Indicate horns for cattle; rub
    lamb's back.)*
smiled down on the baby and watched him, asleep.
(Fold hands and rest cheek on them.)

From *Before and After Christmas* by Debbie Trafton
O'Neal, copyright © 1991 Augsburg Fortress.

Continue telling the Christmas story to include
the angels and shepherds. Stop to sing a joyous song
of Christmas such as "Go Tell It on the Mountain" or
"Angels We Have Heard on High." If the children ask
about the Magi, tell them they will hear more about
the visit of the Wise Men to Bethlehem during
another church year season—Epiphany.

activity for young learners

"fan" Christmas tree

Materials needed: green and yellow construction
paper, blue construction paper, small Christmas
stickers, small self-adhesive stars, brown crayon,
staplers.

"Fan" Christmas tree

Young children can enjoy making a Christmas
tree as a symbol of God's everlasting love for us.

Give each child a piece of green construction
paper. Help them fold the paper into a fan in 1"
folds, starting with the 9" side of the paper. Staple
all layers together at one end. At the other end, fan
out the paper and staple it to the sheet of blue
construction paper as shown in the illustration.

When the tree is in place, children can use stickers
and stars to decorate their own trees.

Make a star out of yellow construction paper to
glue at the top of the tree. Use a brown crayon to
draw a trunk at the bottom.

Say: **The Christmas trees we have in our homes
at Christmas are always green as they grow. Their
branches never change colors. Evergreen trees are a
symbol at Christmas of God's ever present love for
us. God's love never changes.** Read John 3:16 to the
group. Tell the children that that is reason, not only
for trees, but for all of us to sing for joy!

activity for middlers

freeze frame stories

Materials needed: Christmas costumes and props,
camera and film.
Preparation: Bring sheets, costumes, shepherds'
staffs, and other Christmas story props.

Here's an opportunity for older children to do
"freeze frames" of the Christmas story that can be
used as a picture book for younger children or as
greetings for homebound members of your church.

As a group, read the Christmas story from Luke
2:1-20 and also Matthew 1:18—2:12, or use one of
the many beautifully illustrated Christmas books
telling the story of Christ's birth.

Ask children to decide together how many still-
life scenes or "freeze frames" they would need to
create the story. List the scenes on a chalkboard or
poster board for all to see. Ask for volunteers to
play the characters in each scene. Have them create
costumes from the things you brought.

Set up one scene at a time in front of a blank wall
or other plain background. All who are not "actors"
can help compose the scene. Take a photograph of
the scene, then move to the next scene until the
entire story has been told.

Let children use their creativity in showing the story. For example, the angel Gabriel may need to stand on a chair over Mary and Joseph holding a star.

Don't overlook the possibility of a real baby for baby Jesus! A family with a new baby might be honored to visit your class and participate. Remember to send copies of your "freeze frames" to them when the project is finished.

Make sure all have opportunities to be in some of the scenes. If central characters such as Mary and Joseph are different people in each scene, try to maintain the same costumes throughout the scenes.

After the pictures are developed, they can be mounted on sheets of construction paper or placed in an inexpensive photo album to create "The Christmas Story" as told by your class. Or mount the pictures on folded cardstock and make freeze-frame Christmas cards with a photo on the front to give to homebound members of your church from your class.

all together now
Intergenerational session for Christmas

welcome!

Materials needed: green construction paper, markers, tape, one large red construction paper heart.
Preparation: Cut the paper into half-sheets, about 9" x 6". Make a red paper heart for the top of the handprint tree. On the heart print "Gifts from the Heart." Choose a place well traveled during the Christmas season to display the tree.

Greet everyone and give each one a piece of green paper. Ask them to trace and cut handprints.

Ask each person to print his or her name and list a "gift from the heart" on the handprint, gifts that are free or inexpensive, but are also priceless gifts like smiles or hugs.

When the name and "gift from the heart" is written on the handprints, curl the fingers of the paper around a pencil to make them curve slightly like evergreen branches. Place handprints on the wall starting at the bottom and working up to the top in an evergreen tree shape. At the top of the tree, place the red heart made in advance.

explore the story

Materials needed: copies of page 54, narrow curling ribbon, markers, scissors, paper punches.
Preparation: Make photocopies of page 54 on cardstock or other heavy paper (enlarge as desired with your photocopier), one copy for each family or group. Have some extra sheets for individuals within groups who may want to take home a set of figures.

Gather participants and read or tell the Christmas story from Luke 2:1-20 or a Christmas storybook. For adults in the group, the story of Jesus' birth may be an old favorite. For young children who have been around for only four or five Christmas seasons, it may still be a new story.

Give each small group or family a copy of page 54. Ask them to decorate the figures with markers, keeping the words visible, and cut out the figures.

Say: **These figures from the nativity scene have good news to tell. Work together to put the words together in a sentence. Here's a hint: The angel starts the good news.**

Give groups a few minutes to unscramble the sentence, then ask all who are able to read to speak the sentence together.

Cut a piece of ribbon about one yard in length for each group. Ask them to punch a hole at the top of each figure and string each figure onto the ribbon, knotting them in place, spacing figures about 3" apart.

Optional: To make this more active, before stringing the figures ask one adult or older youth per group to be the "Christmas tree" for their group. Ask those people to take the ribbon and move to a spot across the room from the rest of their teams. The goal of each group is to move, relay style, one by one with each nativity piece to the "Christmas tree." When the first person gets to the tree person, the pair ties the angel figure to the ribbon. When it is tied on, the first person moves back to the group, sending the next person to the "tree," and so on to tie figures onto the ribbon at 3" intervals. Continue until all pieces make the sentence complete on the ribbon. When the sentence is complete, the last person can drape the ribbon across the "tree's" shoulders to let all know that the good news is now complete!

When all have finished, encourage them to take the "good news" ribbons home and place them on their real tree for the rest of the Christmas season!

action for all

Christmas Prayer Chain

Materials needed: white construction paper, stapler, markers.

Preparation: Cut paper into 1½" x 9" strips. Have a pattern of a large star available for tracing.

We often link paper chains with the Advent season as a way to wait for Christmas to come. This paper chain will instead be a Christmas prayer chain, reminding all that Christmas lasts for a full 12 days, not just a single evening or a day.

Say: **At home you may be receiving Christmas cards from people you love. Each link of your chain will be a reminder to pray for some of those people each day.**

Give each group or individual 12 paper strips. Ask them to print names or draw faces on each strip to remind them of some of the people who have sent them Christmas greetings. More than one name can be on each strip, but names should be written on only one side of the paper.

Staple the strips into links and join the links into a 12-link chain.

Cut a star from yellow construction paper. Fasten the paper chain to the star.

Say: **Place this chain in a place where you pray. It will be your Christmas prayer chain. The first day of Christmas, pray for the people listed on the first link of your chain. The next day when you pray, add prayers for the people named on the second link plus those from the first link. Continue adding people throughout the 12 days of Christmas. By Epiphany you will see how many people God has given to you as family and friends.**

Las Posadas

Preparation: Ask a few people to create a surprise "party" of Christmas treats and music in a room large enough for the group. If necessary, they may need to hide the treats until the group has gone for their "travels," then quickly assemble the party while the rest are moving around the building.

Explain the "Las Posadas" tradition to the group. Las Posadas begins nine days before Christmas in Hispanic cultures. People become "travelers" who go from door to door, just as Mary and Joseph did, to find a place to stay. Each household they come to gives the same answer, "There's no room." On Christmas Eve they travel once again, asking for a place to stay. Finally they are warmly welcomed to a great party in honor of the Christ child.

Post volunteers at various rooms around the church to give the answer, "There's no room!" as the group of "travelers" arrive at their door.

Take the rest of the group traveling from door to door. Sing a verse of a Christmas carol at each door, then move on. Finally end at the place where the party has been prepared and hear the glad sound, "Welcome!" as everyone enters for treats and song.

Name him Jesus

There are so many wonderful songs of Christmas and each one of them gives many names for the Christ child, Jesus.

Ask a musician to come and lead a sing-along of Christmas carols. Take requests from the group.

Say: **We hear many titles and names given to Jesus at Christmas. When you choose a song for us, also choose one of the names for Jesus given in the song as a "standing name." Whenever we sing that name in the song we will all stand up.** Even young children who cannot read will enjoy listening for the one "standing name" in each song.

6

Epiphany

for leaders

did you know...?

T he season of Epiphany begins on January 6, after the 12 days of Christmas. It ends on the Tuesday before Ash Wednesday.

🌀 "Epiphany" means to show forth or reveal. During Epiphany our Bible readings in worship feature the teachings, miracles, and beginning of Jesus' ministry, revealing to us Jesus as God's only Son.

🌀 Some countries celebrate Epiphany with festive foods such as a King's Cake. Cakes like these have nuts or coins hidden inside. The ones who find the hidden items are the "kings" or "wise ones" for the day.

🌀 Legends of the Star Man in Poland and La Befana in Italy are two of the many characters who give gifts to children at Epiphany, reminiscent of the Magi or Wise Men giving gifts to Jesus.

look it up!

Read the key stories of the Epiphany season in the Bible.

Matthew 2:1-12
Matthew 3:13-17
Matthew 17:1-13

symbols of the season

White is the color for the Epiphany of Our Lord (January 6), the Baptism of Our Lord (the first Sunday after the Epiphany) and the Transfiguration of Our Lord (the last Sunday after the Epiphany). The other Sundays during the Epiphany season use green, the color of growth, as knowledge about Jesus' teachings and miracles spreads.

Star A star that appeared at Jesus' birth guided the Wise Men—or Magi—on their search for the new King, Jesus. The Son of God gives light to all people living in darkness.

Globe The Wise Men came to Bethlehem from afar. They were seeking Jesus, signifying that God sent Jesus for the peoples of all nations. Jesus brings all people together from the east and west, north and south.

Three crowns The three crowns remind us that everyone from humble shepherds to the Wise Men came to find the real King, Jesus.

a bulletin board for Epiphany

Materials needed: gold wrapping paper, poster board, markers.

Preparation: Cover a bulletin board with gold paper and add the heading, "Come and See...Jesus, the Light of the World." Draw a very large five-pointed star on the poster board and cut it out. On the center of the back side of the star, write Matthew 2:1-12. On the back side of each point of the star, write one of the Bible references listed below. Cut the star into six puzzle pieces so that each of the points and the middle of the star is a piece.

Gather a group of learners to help you construct the bulletin board.

Say: **Epiphany is a season when Jesus is revealed to us piece by piece. First we hear the story of the Wise Men who recognize Jesus as "king of the Jews"** (Matthew 2:1-12). **Then comes Jesus' baptism, the beginning of his earthly ministry** (Matthew 3:13-17). **During the following Sundays we read about firsts: Jesus' first miracles** (John 2:1-11 or Mark 1:40-45); **the calling of the first disciples** (Luke 5:1-11); **Jesus' first teaching in the synagogue**

Epiphany puzzle bulletin board

(Luke 4:14-21); **and finally the Transfiguration, the glorious revelation of Jesus as God's beloved Son** (Mark 9:2-9).

Give the puzzle pieces to six individuals or small groups. Ask them to draw a picture of the Bible passage listed on the back of the piece.

Put only one piece on the bulletin board each week during the Epiphany season, starting with the center piece of the visit of the Wise Men.

Talk with the children about how people learned about Jesus a little at a time. Help them to imagine each story of the Epiphany season as another spotlight that shines on Jesus, showing us more and more of who Jesus is, until Transfiguration Sunday when all of the lights come on as Jesus stands with Moses and Elijah on the mountain! Then we hear God's words, similar to Jesus' baptism, "This is my Son, the Beloved; listen to him!" (Mark 9:7).

Sunday school opening

Preparation: Place a globe or map in the Worship Box. (If you have not made a Worship Box, see page 5 for instructions.) Wrap a candle in yellow or gold wrapping paper, then place it in a box, wrap the box as a present and put it in the Worship Box. Optional: Have self-adhesive stars for each child.

Gather the children and take the wrapped present out of the Worship Box.

Say: **Christmas Day was ___ days ago. During Christmas we saw many of these.** (Hold up the wrapped package.) **How many presents do you still have wrapped at home now?** (Accept responses.)

Why don't we want to leave presents lying around wrapped up? (We want to see what's in them, couldn't use them if they're wrapped up, and so on.)

We have entered a new season at church. It's called Epiphany. At the beginning of the Epiphany season we hear a lot about some special people who brought gifts to Jesus, not exactly like this one, but very precious gifts. What can you tell me about them? (The Wise Men, or Magi, came from the East, followed the star to Jesus, tricked King Herod, and other story details.)

You may wish to read Matthew 2:1-12 to the group.

Say: **To remember the gifts brought to Jesus by the Wise Men, we give gifts to each other at Christmas. We can't give gifts to Jesus in the same way the Wise Men did. We give gifts to each other instead to share the joy and excitement about Jesus' birth with them. Who would like to unwrap this present?** (Accept help from a volunteer.)

Before opening the box, ask: **Now the paper is off. Would we know what the present is if we left it in the box?** (No.) **Remember that during Epiphany. We wouldn't know very much about Jesus if we left his story back at the manger. Epiphany stories help tell us more about Jesus: what he did, where he went, and who he was. He was God's Son!**

Open up the box and remove the wrapped candle. Show it to the children. Say: **Now we're getting closer. At least we know what shape our present is! That gives us a hint about what it might be.** (Children can make guesses of a stick, a baton, a candle, and so on.) After guesses are made, unwrap the present and light the candle.

Continue: **During the Epiphany season of our church year, we get hints about who Jesus is. There can be as many as nine Sundays during the Epiphany season. On the final Sunday of Epiphany, we finally get to see Jesus in bright white light on a mountain as God commands, "This is my beloved Son. Listen to him!" That's when we finally know what a bright light Jesus is for our lives. And the best part of the gift? Jesus comes not just for us, but for the whole world.** (Bring out the globe or map.)

Sing songs about stars and light such as "This Little Light of Mine," "We Three Kings," or even "Twinkle, Twinkle, Little Star" for young children. If you brought star stickers, place one on each child's shirt.

activity for young learners

chalk prints

Materials needed: white construction paper, plain white paper, colored chalk, facial tissue, removable tape.

Preparation: Cut assorted Epiphany symbols as well as a cross and a heart out of plain paper, making one symbol that is about 10" tall for each child. Cut a few others about 2" to 3" tall.

Ask the children to sit at tables and give each one a piece of white construction paper. Bring out the symbols made in advance and tell the children about each one. Ask each child to choose one symbol to use first on their paper.

Place the symbol in the center of the page, tacking it down in two or three places with small pieces of removable tape.

Say: **To make Epiphany pictures today you will use chalk. In parts of eastern Europe, families mark the doorways of their homes with chalk like this:** (Print on a chalkboard or black piece of paper the first two numbers of the present year, then C+M+B, finally the last two numbers of the year. For example, 19 C+M+B 99. The initials stand for the legendary names of the Wise Men, Caspar, Melchior, and Balthasar, and also for the Latin phrase "Christ, bless this house.") **They do this to as a sign of blessing for their homes for the coming year. When you take your picture home, you may want to hang it above a door, too, as an Epiphany blessing to your home.**

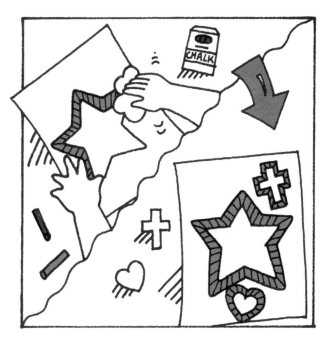

Chalk print

Each child can choose a stick of chalk and, pressing very firmly, use it to color a 1" strip on the cutout symbol. Make the strip go all around the edges of the symbol. Demonstrate how to move the chalk from the center to the edge of the symbol to prevent tearing.

After coloring, show how to rub the chalk out onto the white sheet. If darker colors of chalk were used, rub the chalk out onto the white sheet with a tissue or with thumbs. If lighter colors of chalk are used, rub with thumbs instead of tissue to make the color more vibrant.

When the rubbing is completed, remove the symbol sheet, and an outline on the full sheet should be visible.

Children can use a smaller symbol and repeat the process to add more designs to their papers if they like.

activity for middlers

pinwheel stars

Materials needed: 4" squares of construction paper in two contrasting colors, glue sticks, white glue, glitter, cotton swabs, metallic curling gift-wrap ribbon, sharp scissors, paper punch.

Each Epiphany star is made from two pinwheels glued back to back. To make one pinwheel, use a

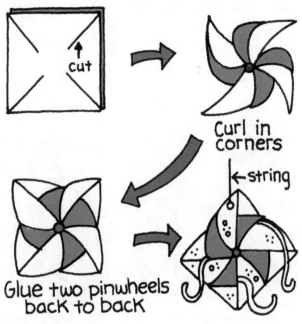

Pinwheel star

glue stick to glue two construction paper squares of different colors to each other. Cut a straight line in toward the center from each corner of the square, stopping about 1" from the center of the square. (You may want to use a ruler to draw lines for cutting.) Pull every other corner to the center, being careful not to crease the paper. Secure the four corners in the center with glue, holding until the glue dries. (You may also use a stapler for this.) Decorate the pinwheels by applying dots of glue with a cotton swab, then sprinkling glitter on the wet glue.

When the pinwheels are dry, glue them together back to back. Hold until the glue dries. Punch several holes around the edges of the star and attach curled metallic gift-wrap ribbon streamers. Attach one uncurled ribbon to use for hanging the star.

all together now
Intergenerational session for Epiphany

welcome!

Preparation: Find four Bibles and make bookmarks listing the following four passages for four readers. Reader 1, Isaiah 43:1,5a (east); Reader 2, Isaiah 43:5b (west); Reader 3, Isaiah 43:6a (north); Reader 4, Isaiah 43:6b-7 (south).

Welcome all to the Epiphany event. As a way to let participants interact, begin with a game. By the end of the game, all participants should be joined together in one long chain.

Begin by asking all in the group to make a large standing circle in an open area. Ask for four volunteers to read the passages from Isaiah in order. Try to find readers who are standing on the north, south, east, and west sides of the circle.

Say: **During this season of Epiphany we think about the ways God gives a very special gift, his own Son Jesus, to people of all nations. God is with us. God has called each one of us by name, just as he called Jesus by name as his beloved Son at his baptism.**

In this game you will be called by name by the Epiphany Chain. This chain begins with only two people. (Ask for volunteers or select people to come to the center with you.)

When I say "Epiphany" the game will begin. The chain will move as quickly as it can to latch onto another person's shoulders. When the chain finds another "link" it names that person and changes direction. Now the last person in the chain becomes the first. The Epiphany Chain will continue adding links and changing direction until all are connected. For those of you who are loose links, you may move quickly trying not to attach.

Play the game until all are connected in one long Epiphany Chain.

explore the story

Materials needed: Bibles; props and costumes (optional).

Divide the groups evenly into six drama teams. Include persons of all ages on each team. Ask each team to spend three minutes preparing to dramatize one of the following Bible passages highlighted in worship during the season of Epiphany:

Matthew 2:1-12, The visit of the Wise Men
Matthew 3:13-17, Jesus' baptism
John 2:1-11 or Mark 1:40-45, Jesus' first miracles
Luke 5:1-11, The calling of the first disciples
Luke 4:14-21, Jesus' teaching in the synagogue
Mark 9:2-9, The Transfiguration

Say: **During the weeks of Epiphany we learn a lot about the baby Jesus, born in Bethlehem. We hear about events that reveal who Jesus is. Each one of the stories turns the lights on brighter to let us see Jesus as God's Son, the Savior of all nations. You will be in the spotlight today to act out some of those important Bible stories.**

Give the groups time to prepare their drama. Encourage everyone to take part in some way, even as the water at Jesus' baptism, the wine jars at Cana, or Moses and Elijah at the transfiguration. Encourage imagination and enjoyment of the stories!

When the stories are ready, present them in the order listed above. You may even want to videotape your Epiphany Players and let them see themselves as Epiphany "stars"!

action for all

Spinning a yarn

Materials needed: balls of yarn.

In a large open area ask everyone to sit in a circle. If you are a large group, consider splitting into two or three groups, each in their own circle.

This activity will give people opportunity to hear from each other about other countries. Ask the groups, "If you could leave this afternoon to visit any place in the world, where would you go and why?"

Give a ball of yarn to one person in the circle. After that person has answered, he or she holds one end of the yarn and tosses the ball across the circle to another person, and so on. Always toss the yarn across the circle to make points of a star, each person holding on to their own piece of yarn after they have answered. When finished, hold the yarn close to the floor to notice the many-pointed star created by the group.

Many lands, many voices

Preparation: Invite guest musicians to your inter-generational event to lead and give background information on songs about Jesus that originate in a variety of countries.

Epiphany is a wonderful time to meet Christians from all nations, even if only through their music. Choose global songs that are favorites in your congregation. Tell the participants a little about the song or the culture that it comes from before singing each one. Teach one or two of the songs and enjoy a sing-along.

Stellar treats

Preparation: If your event is in the evening, you may wish to expand the treats into a "world tour" supper. Invite people to bring and share a food from their own culture or one their family enjoys eating. It may turn into a smorgasbord of tastes that will be an annual Epiphany tradition. For a simpler snack, have a volunteer bake some kind of spice cake with three coins wrapped in foil, baked inside to resemble a King's Cake. Or have someone make Epiphany Bread for the group. The recipe is found on page 55 of this book.

Sharing food is another way of using all the senses to experience the season of Epiphany. Any kind of bread or cake with three hidden almonds or coins (wrapped in foil before baking) can be considered a King's cake. All ages will wonder who will be the three "wise ones" for the day!

The Epiphany Bread recipe has proven to be a favorite with young and old alike. The spices of cinnamon, nutmeg, and cloves, and the hidden coins give a simple reminder about the gifts from the East brought to Jesus by the Wise Men. Make copies of the recipe on page 55 for those who would like to try it at home.

Before enjoying an Epiphany snack together, pray a prayer of thanksgiving and a prayer for the sharing of the gospel with all people:

Generous God, you have come to us in Jesus, the light of the world. As this food and drink give us refreshment, strengthen us by your Spirit, that as your baptized sons and daughters we may share your light with all the world. Grant this through Christ our Lord. Amen

From *Come, Lord Jesus* by Susan Briehl, copyright © 1996 Augsburg Fortress.

As people leave, thank them for participating in an Epiphany event for all senses and for all in the family of God.

7

Lent

for leaders

did you know...?

The word *lent* comes from a Latin word *lencten* meaning "springtime." As God's creation wakes up after a cold winter season in many areas of the country, Lent is a time for rebirth and new starts. As the days "lengthen," also a part of the meaning of the word *lent,* we move from darkness to light just as we move from Lent to Easter.

- The season from Ash Wednesday to Easter is 40 days, not counting Sundays. Sundays are considered "little Easters," and are not counted in the 40 days.

- In the early church, Lent was the time to prepare candidates for Baptism. The new Christians would then be baptized on the evening before Easter at the Easter Vigil.

- The 40 days of Lent are symbolic of other biblical journeys: Jesus' 40 days in the wilderness; Moses and the Israelites wandering 40 years in the wilderness; Noah's ark in the rainstorm for 40 days and 40 nights; Elijah's journey to Mt. Horeb; Jonah in 40 days of penance with the people of Nineveh.

- Fasting or other sacrifices are often practiced during Lent to help us remember Jesus' great sacrifice for all generations.

- Ash Wednesday is the first day of Lent. The ashes—often made from burning the palm fronds from the previous Palm Sunday—traced in the form of a cross on our foreheads on Ash Wednesday are reminders of our own sins and our short lives that must be placed in God's hands. "You are dust, and to dust you shall return" (Genesis 3:19).

look it up

Review the biblical account of Jesus' final days of earthly ministry, suffering, and death to better understand the season of Lent.

Matthew 26 and Matthew 27
Mark 14 and Mark 15
Luke 22 and Luke 23
John 18 and John 19

symbols of the season

The color given to the season of Lent is purple. Purple is the color for royalty, for Jesus, who rode into Jerusalem as king and was mocked as the "King of the Jews" on Good Friday.

Purple is also a color of penitence, which is a constant theme throughout Lent for all Christians as we remember our sins for which Jesus died on the cross.

Black, or an absence of color, is used on Good Friday, when the death of Christ seems to make all of life vacant and colorless. Some churches also use black on Ash Wednesday.

Crosses Crosses in Jesus' day were instruments of death. Today an empty cross points us to a risen Lord. Even during Lent, the end and also the beginning of life is visible on that cross.

Chalice and bread The chalice of wine and loaf of bread are symbols of Jesus' last supper with his disciples, commemorated on the Thursday before Easter, Maundy Thursday.

Palm branches Leafy branches, likely palms, were used to line the path for Jesus' triumphal entry into Jerusalem for his final week leading up to the cross.

Crown of thorns The soldiers taking Jesus to the cross mocked him by placing a crown of thorns on his head.

Foot and footwashing In the gospel text read on Maundy Thursday, Jesus gives his disciples a new commandment, "Love one another as I have loved you." Symbolic of the Christian life of service, Jesus washed the disciples' feet. (See John 13:1-14,34-35.) Maundy comes from the Latin word *maundatum* meaning "commandment."

Feet also remind us of the journey we travel through the season of Lent, through the valley of death to new life.

a banner for Lent

Materials needed: crayons, white cotton fabric about 24" x 36", wide adhesive tape (such as masking or duct tape), iron, chart paper, dowel rod, glue, purple fringe (optional).

Ordinary crayon can be used to make a batik style banner, making it possible for children to help create it.

Using the adhesive tape, make a wide cross in the center of the banner. Then have children use purple, black, brown, and other dark colors of crayons to color out from the edge of the tape onto the fabric. Press firmly while using the crayons and go over the area a few times to make the color vivid.

Make the outline of lettering with pencil on the banner. In the upper left corner print the word "Once..." In the lower right corner print "...and for ALL."

Crayon batik banner

Have the children use purple crayon to fill in the lettering.

When the coloring is finished, remove the tape from the cross. Lay the banner with crayon side down on a flat surface covered with chart paper or other similar paper. Iron over the back of the banner on the colored areas, adding clean paper until color no longer comes off the banner.

Glue or sew a pocket along the top border to insert a dowel rod for hanging. Add purple fringe to the bottom of the banner, if desired.

Sunday school opening

Preparation: Cut white paper or fabric into 8" squares, one per learner. Make one "alleluia square" in advance. If you have not prepared a Worship Box, see page 5 for instructions.

As the children come, ask them to form a line behind you and walk, "follow the leader" style. Vary your walking pace—a slow burdened pace, a springy step, a parade march. Ask the children to sit down.

Say: **There is a church year season that comes every spring that we call "Lent." During Lent, we hear many stories about Jesus, some very happy and some very sad. Some people like to think of the season of Lent as a "journey," a time to travel through the Bible stories of Jesus' ministry on earth. On Ash Wednesday, we might feel like we are carrying a big load as we remember the wrongs we have done. On Palm Sunday, we might feel like marching and jumping for joy with the crowd. And on Good Friday, we walk very slowly and quietly as we remember how Jesus died for us.**

Some people give up something or make a change during Lent. (Ask children for things their families are already doing.) **Here at church we are going to give up a word, the word *alleluia*. Alleluia!** (say it with enthusiasm) **is a word that sounds like a celebration. When we remember how Jesus suffered and died, we don't have a reason to celebrate. We will wait for a celebration until the big surprise and joy of Easter comes!**

Show the children a piece of fabric or paper, made in advance, with the word "alleluia" printed on it. Place it in the Worship Box.

Give each child a piece of paper or fabric and ask the children to make their own "alleluia square" in class, then add their squares to the Worship Box as they remember to put away the alleluias from their everyday lives during Lent.

Sing a song that tells of Jesus' love and sacrifice for us, such as "Were You There"; then pray the Lord's Prayer together. For young children it would be helpful to pray each petition slowly, then ask the children to echo you after each petition throughout the prayer.

Preparation for Easter: If the Easter Sunday school opening activity will be used during the Easter season, ask a volunteer to add some glittery gold fabric paint or glitter glue to each alleluia square after children have placed their squares in the Worship Box. When dry, return them to the box.

activity for young learners

Lenten laces

Materials needed: shoelace or non-fraying cord, about 9" per child; one purple, red, gold/yellow, and green bead per child.

The colored beads of Lenten laces help children remember the stories of Jesus. You may want to do this activity over a period of four Sundays, adding one bead each week.

Give each child a lace or cord with a knot 4" from the end.

String a purple bead for Jesus, the King. Tell the children about Jesus' entry into Jerusalem on Palm Sunday.

String a red bead for Jesus who died for all. Talk about Good Friday at a level appropriate for the children. Explain that the red bead is for Jesus' blood, his suffering and death.

Say: **Jesus died on the cross on a Friday, and every year we remember his death on the day we call Good Friday. The word "good" comes from an English word that means "god." We can think of this day as "God's Friday." Thinking about Jesus' death doesn't make Good Friday a happy day. But we know that because God loves us so very much, he gave his only Son, Jesus, to save us from our sins. Our faith in this turns a sad Friday into Good Friday.**

Read John 3:16. Ask the children to say it with you, phrase by phrase. Or learn a song with John 3:16 as the text.

String a golden bead for the bright light of the angel at the empty Easter morning tomb. Share the Easter story in brief with the children in a way that

sounds like you are sharing a secret with them, with more to come at Easter!

String a green bead for the new life we are given through Jesus' resurrection.

Say: **We are all given new life because Jesus died and rose again on Easter. Imagine that this green bead is a little seed that will grow and grow and grow. That's like what God's love can do, too. It can grow in us every day, so we can know God's love and share it with others.**

Make another knot to hold the beads in place and tie the Lenten lace on your wrist.

Say: **When others ask you about the beads, tell them the stories of Jesus!**

Optional: Children may want to wear their Lenten beads on their shoes instead of on their wrists. If they are wearing tie shoes, they could remove one shoelace and place the beads in the center of the lace, then lace it back into the shoe again. What a great way to "walk" the journey with Jesus through Lent!

activity for middlers

crown of thorns

Materials needed: black construction paper, copies of the daily reading strips on page 56, scissors, tape.

Preparation: Make a copy of page 56 for each learner. Cut three 4½" x 12" construction paper strips for each child. Make one crown of thorns as an example.

Give each child three strips of black paper. Ask the children to stack the three strips, then accordion-

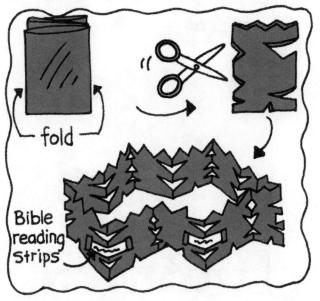

Crown of thorns

fold them into fourths. Demonstrate how to cut through all layers on the folds from both sides being careful to leave some of each folded edge uncut. Since this is to be a crown of thorns, strive for rough edges and sharp cuts.

Read Matthew 27:27-29 to explain the significance of the crown of thorns.

Unfold the strips and tape them together to make a circular crown shape. Tape one of the Bible reading slips from page 56 to each of the six "panels."

Encourage the children to place the crown of thorns on their table at home and read from their Bibles at a family table time, either once a week during Lent or each day during Holy Week.

all together now
Intergenerational session for Lent

welcome!

Materials needed: washable ink pads, 8½" x 11" plain white paper cut in quarters (4¼" x 5½").

Greet everyone and invite each person to make a footprint name tag.

Make a fist with one hand and press the little finger side of the hand into the ink pad. With the fist still clenched, press the ink onto the name tag. The image should look like a small footprint. Press the tip of your finger into the ink and use it to make five toes above the "footprint" on the name tag.

Now each person can add his or her name to the name tag.

When the name tags are finished, sing songs that refer to a journey or to walking such as "I Want Jesus to Walk with Me," "Just a Closer Walk with Thee," or "We Are Marching in the Light of God."

explore the story

Say: **When you came in today each one of you made a footprint. It's probably about the size of the footprint you would have made when you first learned how to walk. Imagine how many steps you have taken since then!**

Lent is a time when Christians think about their walk with God each day. Sometimes we walk through happy days, sometimes the days become difficult and dark. The writer of Psalm 23 talks about that. Read Psalm 23, then ask the group for examples of happy days and difficult days.

Say: **Jesus had the same kinds of days we do, some happy days and some difficult days. He spent 40 days in the wilderness fasting as he prepared to do his ministry. That's one reason we have 40 days of Lent before Easter.**

During these 40 days of Lent, we remember the happy day in Jesus' life when he rode a donkey into Jerusalem; and we remember the very dark day that Jesus died. Throughout Lent, Christians "walk through" the stories of Jesus' life and death. As we go, we remember that God is always with us.

That's why we often take extra time to pray during Lent. In the early church, people who were not yet baptized spent all of Lent praying, fasting, and learning more about Jesus. That was their Lenten walk. What can you do during Lent that will help you walk closer to God? You might think of things you can give up for 40 days. Making sacrifices is a small way of remembering the sacrifice Jesus made for us on the cross. You may also think of extra things you might add to your days such as a Lenten family prayer time.

Ask participants to meet in small groups to share ideas for their own Lenten walks.

action for all

Try setting up these Lenten activities as stations, allowing participants to move at their own pace or do them as a group.

Palm crosses

Materials needed: palm branches or strips of paper ½" x 12" and ½" x 9".

Preparation: If you have real palm fronds to use, moisten them to make them pliable. Tear the palm fronds into ½" strips of 12" and 9" lengths. Each person will need a 12" and a 9" strip of paper or palm leaf.

Palm crosses are a simple yet fitting Lenten symbol. Encourage participants of different ages to work on the crosses together, so they can help each other. Once the pattern is learned, even young children will be able to fold the crosses together to make bookmarks or Lenten decorations for use at home. Since they are so lightweight they would also be a fine thing to tuck into a letter to a faraway relative or friend or a person who is homebound.

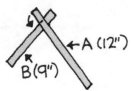

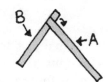

1. Place strip A over strip B as shown. Fold end of A back.

2. Fold end of strip B back also.

3. Take other end of B and bring around and push through top slot. Pull it completely down.

4. Take end of A and push back through back slot. Pull it completely up.

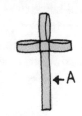

5. Slide end of B through top loop. Then double back halfway and tuck end inside slot.

6. Take end of A and slide it through back slot until top of cross forms.

7. Fold bottom of A in half and tuck its end into back slot. You're done!

Palm cross

Follow the steps shown in the diagram. When finishing the last steps, the ends of the palm strips may need to be cut to fit inside the folds of the cross.

Potpourri fit for a king

Materials needed: colorful fabric scraps, at least 6" square; ¼ cup per person of a mixture of dried citrus peel and kitchen spices such as rosemary, fennel, cinnamon, allspice, and cloves (or ready-made scented potpourri); thin ribbon in 12" lengths.

The phrase "fit for a king" usually means the best quality. Read Matthew 2:11, Matthew 26:6-13, and Luke 23:50-56. People brought spices and other rare oils to Jesus as an infant, at supper with the disciples, and after his death. They did this out of respect for their King, even though he never had a royal throne or palace like other kings.

Make potpourri pouches as a Lenten remembrance. The little bags can be given away or kept near other Lenten symbols at home.

Ask each person to cut a 6" fabric circle by trimming off the corners of the fabric squares.

Mix the spices in a large bowl.

Scoop out about ¼ cup of the potpourri and place it on the wrong side of the fabric circle. Bring the edges together and fasten with a decorative piece of ribbon.

Pretzels and prayers

Materials needed: dough for pretzel making (refrigerated or frozen bread dough for rolls); coarse salt; beaten egg; cookie sheets; plastic gloves for food preparation.

Preparation: Thaw frozen bread dough. Preheat the oven to 400° F.

Did you know that pretzels are a Lenten food? Long ago they were made by monks as a bread they called *bracalle*, or "little arms," to symbolize arms folded in prayer. In Germany the bread was called *brezel*, which to us became *pretzel*.

Cut each roll of thawed dough into two pieces. Give each person a plate as a working space. Roll the dough into ropes ¼"-½" in diameter. Twist the ropes into pretzel shapes.

Place the pretzels on greased cookie sheets. Brush with egg and sprinkle with coarse salt. Bake at 400° F for 12 minutes or until golden brown.

When pretzels are cool enough to eat, ask participants to all fold their arms "pretzel style" across their chests for a table prayer, then enjoy the snack together.

A prayer station

Modern life seems to be constantly moving and even prayer time is often swallowed up by pressing needs during the day. Give participants a quiet place in your church's chapel or even an empty classroom to go and spend a few minutes in prayer. Place Lenten symbols on a table covered with purple cloth. Provide a Bible with pages marked for the passion story of Jesus.

8
Easter

for leaders

did you know...?

Easter is the oldest festival of the church year. It can occur anytime between March 22 and April 25. Easter Day is set as the first Sunday following the first full moon after the first day of spring.

- Easter is a time for glorious changes. The last three days of Holy Week are called the triduum, a "trio of days" extending from Maundy Thursday through Good Friday to Easter. Christians remember Jesus' Last Supper, then the journey to the crucifixion, and finally the good news of Jesus' resurrection at Easter.

- Every Sunday in the church year is proclaimed "a little Easter" since we continue to celebrate Jesus' resurrection at all times.

- In the early Christian church, new Christians were baptized at the Vigil of Easter, the night before Easter. Many churches today celebrate baptisms or renewal of baptismal promises at Easter Vigil services.

- Ascension Day, which marks Jesus' ascension into heaven (Luke 24:44-53), is celebrated 40 days after Easter.

- The Easter season lasts 50 days. Some call these seven weeks from Easter Sunday until the Day of Pentecost a "week of weeks."

look it up

Reread the story of the first Easter in the Bible.
Matthew 28:1-10
Mark 16:1-8
Luke 24: 1-12
John 20:1-10

symbols of the season

White is the color for the seven weeks of the Easter season—a color of purity, newness, and joy. Gold is often added on Easter Day, the most holy and festive of all days in the Christian church.

Butterfly The butterfly symbolizes new life because of how it emerges in a changed form from its chrysalis.

Lily The lily and many other spring flowers grow from bulbs that must be planted in the ground before their new life can begin.

Empty tomb The empty tomb and the empty cross proclaim, "Jesus is not here. He is risen!"

Crown The crown of thorns has now become a crown of glory for the risen Lord.

Egg Whether elaborately decorated or plainly dyed at home, Easter eggs have come to symbolize the sealed tomb with new life waiting to break out.

a bulletin board for Easter

Materials needed: white paper to cover bulletin board, computer banner or sign displaying the words of 2 Corinthians 5:17, paper egg cartons, chenille strips, paint, bright colors of tissue paper.

Begin a bulletin board for the Easter season on Palm Sunday by covering the board with white paper. At the top of the bulletin board, mount a computer banner or sign with the Bible verse, "So if anyone is in Christ, there is a new creation: everything old has passed away; see, everything has become new!" (2 Corinthians 5:17).

Enlist children to help make caterpillars to put on the bulletin board. Cut paper egg cartons into strips of three "bumps." Paint the caterpillar bodies black

So if anyone is in Christ, there is a new creation: everything old has passed away; see, everything has become new!

2 Corinthians 5:17

Easter bulletin board

or dark green. When the paint has dried, hold the egg carton caterpillar, bumpy side up, and make a face on the top of the first bump with marker or crayon, then punch a chenille strip through the carton above the face to form the caterpillar's antennae. Pin the caterpillars to the bulletin board at least 12" apart.

Before Easter morning, cut 12" circles of gold, yellow, or other brightly colored tissue paper or iridescent wrapping paper and gather each circle together in the middle, fastening it together with a twist tie to make butterfly wings. Very early on Easter morning, or the evening before, place the wings behind the middle bump of the caterpillars and reattach the newly made butterflies.

On or after Easter, talk with the children about the Bible verse on the board. In what other ways are they reminded of Jesus' resurrection in the spring? (Flowers from bulbs or seeds, chicks and birds from eggs, green grass and buds from bare branches in northern climates.)

Sunday school opening

Preparation: If the children created "alleluia squares" at the beginning of Lent (see page 35), place them in the Worship Box. (If you have not made a Worship Box, see page 5 for instructions.) Also place symbols of Baptism in the box, such as a shell, a baptismal candle, or a baptismal gown. Add a sticker

with some kind of Easter symbol (butterfly, egg, crown) for each child or an ink stamp and washable ink stamp pad. Then stuff the box with colorful tissue paper so that the box is overflowing with the lid placed loosely on top.

As the children gather today, welcome them with an exuberant "Happy Easter!" as you bring out the Worship Box.

Say: **Look at the box today: It is so full that it's opening by itself! Easter is such a joyful time, we can't keep the news hidden. Jesus is risen! Let's see if we can find a way to unbox some of that excitement.**

Pull out the colorful paper and finally the "alleluia squares."

Say: **Here they are! This is exactly what we need for today. Remember that we put our alleluias away for Lent so we could remember the sad times for Jesus and his followers, especially Jesus' death on the cross. But now we have heard the rest of the story: Jesus did not stay in the tomb. He is risen! The alleluias can't stay in the box anymore. They need to be sung and spoken often during these Easter days.** If the children made these squares during Lent, return them now to each child.

Sing songs that contain lots of "alleluias," such as "Jesus Christ Is Risen Today."

After the song, look into the Worship Box and, with a surprised look, let the children know that there is more in the box. Pull out the baptismal symbols. Ask children to identify them and figure out when we use them. (At baptisms.)

Say: **Each one of us celebrates our own "little Easter" at a baptism. In Baptism we are reminded of the new life in Christ that God gives to each one of us. When we are baptized the pastor says, "Child of God, you have been sealed by the Holy Spirit and marked with the cross of Christ forever." Here in the box is a mark to wear today that reminds you of your own "little Easter."**

Give each child a sticker or make a stamp on the children's hands. Tell them what the Easter symbol means as you go from child to child.

End the opening with an Easter prayer. Ask children to respond with a joyful "alleluia!" after each sentence.

Leader: **We praise you, Lord, for the new life of Easter.**
All: **Alleluia!**
Leader: **We praise you, Lord, for our new life in Baptism.**
All: **Alleluia!**
Leader: **We thank you, Lord, for voices to sing Easter joy!**
All: **Alleluia! Amen.**

activity for young learners

creation shakers

Preparation: Plan to take a walk outdoors with your learners to gather nature items such as pebbles, twigs, small pine cones, and seeds. Or gather these items ahead of time. You will need two clear plastic cups (8-10 oz.) per child, colored electrical tape or other stretchable adhesive tape, and assorted Easter stickers.

At Easter, all of creation shouts for joy. Young children can make creation shakers to use as rhythm instruments with Easter songs.

Give each child one plastic cup. Invite the children to choose four or five things from the collected nature items and place them in their cups. Cover the cup with a second cup and tape the two together with colorful tape. Add other bands of tape around the cup, and add stickers for decoration.

Tell the children to listen while you read Psalm 95:1-6 to them. Ask them to listen to find out what

Creation shaker

parts of God's creation are mentioned in the verses. (The earth, mountains, sea, dry land.)

Say: **Especially at Easter, we notice how God's creation seems to be changing. New life is all around us in the flowers popping out of the ground, the new green grass, the baby animals and birds, and the days with more light and less darkness. It's easy to understand how the writer of those Bible verses felt. Let us make a joyful noise, too!**

Invite the children to sing a favorite Easter song and to use their new instruments to accompany the singing.

activity for middlers

alleluia rocks

Materials needed: stones, water-base latex paint, brushes, paint shirts.
Preparation: Collect smooth flat beach stones or light-colored stones used in landscaping. Ask parents for donations of partially used cans of latex paint, exterior or interior.

Older children will enjoy making "alleluia rocks" as surprises of Easter joy.

Read Luke 19:37-40. Ask the children to tell about the verses. What was taking place? (Jesus' entry into Jerusalem on Palm Sunday.) What did the Pharisees want? (They wanted the crowd to stop the shouting.)

Say: **Jesus told the Pharisees that even if the people would stop shouting praises, the stones would shout. Especially when we see new life in creation around Easter time, we are aware that God's creation is saying its own alleluia. Use your imagination and create a face or a bright "alleluia" on one of these rocks that shouts out the good news of Jesus' resurrection.**

Invite the children to choose a rock and create a funny face or their own calligraphy of "alleluia" with water-base latex paint. Provide paint shirts, or garbage bags with cut-out neck holes to protect clothing if necessary.

As the children paint, encourage them to think about the surprise it must have been for Jesus' followers as they met him in various places after the resurrection. (See Luke 24:1-7; Luke 24:13-16, 30-32; Luke 24: 36-39; Matthew 28:8-10; John 20:19-20.) Encourage the children to put themselves in the disciples' place. What would they have done? What would they have recognized about Jesus?

Allow the rocks to dry for a few days. When the children take their rocks home, suggest that they place the rocks in a garden or in an area filled with landscape stones. When people see the painted face or "alleluia," they will get an Easter surprise!

all together now
Intergenerational session for Easter

welcome!

Preparation: Make copies of the sign language for "alleluia" on page 56 for participants.

As participants gather, have music of the Easter season playing, or ask a church musician to come and play for the group. Sing a verse of a song that contains the word *alleluia*. Encourage the younger children to sing the alleluias even if they can't read or don't know the rest of the words.

Teach the sign language for "alleluia" to the group. (See page 56 in this book.)

Once the group has learned the sign, sing the song again or choose another alleluia song. Use the alleluia sign each time "alleluia" is sung.

explore the story

Preparation: Locate plastic Easter eggs and fill each one so that the colors and items filling them match the text of the story. Leave one egg empty and place them all in an Easter basket. Adapt the story to fit other Easter items you would like to include. Save the empty egg for the end of the story. Have a Bible handy, marked at Luke 24:1-12; this is part of the story to be told.

Bring out the basket of eggs for all to see. Invite them to listen as you or another storyteller tells the following story.

The Empty Egg

What a curious thing! The class of Sunday school children came to their classroom one morning to find Easter eggs on the table. They all knew it was too early for Easter.

"Teacher, Easter is still one week away!" said Tom. "Why are there eggs today?"

Their teacher, Mr. Lucas, smiled. "I'd like each one of you to take an egg home."

"Do we hide it?" asked Aaron.

"No, it's not a hiding egg, it's a finding egg. I want you to find something that means 'Easter' to you and put it inside the egg. Bring your eggs back on Easter Sunday and we'll share the surprises."

As the children left that day, they were all talking about what they would bring back. They were filled with ideas for their eggs.

Easter Sunday came and so did the children! Soon the basket was filled with colorful eggs. Mr. Lucas read the Easter story from his Bible, Luke 24:1-12. *(Read the Bible story for the group.)*

"Now let's open the eggs and find out what Easter surprises you have to share." Mr. Lucas picked up the yellow egg.

"That's mine!" said Angela as Mr. Lucas opened the egg. "It's a flower. It reminds me of new life as the seeds begin to grow."

Mr. Lucas next found a purple one. "Open it! It's filled with jelly beans!" burst Tom. "There's enough for everybody. Anything that tastes that good gives me Easter joy!"

"Those candies look like little eggs themselves. That's a symbol of life, too," added Rosa.

Everyone had a chance to tell about their eggs. *(Add additional story characters if you wish to lengthen the story to match the number of eggs in your basket.)*

Finally there was only one egg left. Mr. Lucas opened it, then looked puzzled. He knew it had to be Mark's egg. "Mark, didn't you understand what I said? Your egg is empty. Do you need more time? Maybe we can give you some ideas."

"Oh, no," replied Mark. "I knew right away what to bring."

"But there's nothing there!" someone exclaimed.

"Egg-zactly," said Mark. "Just like the tomb. It was empty on Easter morning. Jesus was alive! That's what's most important to me at Easter."

All agreed. Mark did understand what Easter was all about!

action for all

Try some Easter activities! Set them up as activity stations, allowing participants to move among them at their own pace.

50 ways for 50 days

Materials: chart paper and markers.

Since there are 50 days in the Easter season, ask people to suggest their favorite 50 ways to enjoy the season.

Hang a large piece of chart paper on the wall. Number from 1 to 50 down the left side of the paper. Use the back side, or another piece of paper, as needed. Encourage participants to write down the ways they enjoy God's creation, such as finding the first new flower sprouting in the garden; or ways they experience the new life of resurrection and Baptism, such as a walk in a gentle spring rain, a family outing to the swimming pool, reading the Easter story from a new picture book, and so on.

Make copies of the list available for congregation members during the Easter weeks.

Easter people

Materials needed: eggs, markers, potting soil, grass seed, paper towel tubes.

Preparation: Cut the paper towel tubes into 1" rings.

Say: **Christians are often called Easter people. Jesus' death and resurrection give us hope and forgiveness for a new life, every day.**

Explain how to make "Easter egg people." Break open fresh eggs close to the small end of the egg, leaving most of the shell intact. Empty the eggs into a bowl and save the yolks and whites for a scrambled egg feast later in the session.

Carefully draw a face on the eggshell with colored markers, with the open end up. Set the shell in a paper towel ring and place potting soil in the shell. Moisten the dirt with water.

Sprinkle the grass seed on top of the dirt and cover with plastic wrap. In a few days when the seeds begin sprouting, remove the plastic wrap and place

Easter people

the Easter egg person in the sun. Watch as the grass continues to grow. Children will enjoy giving their characters haircuts as the grass grows!

An Easter feast

Materials needed: eggs (from Easter people activity), utensils, fruit, small plates, forks.

Preparation: Ask someone to be the chef to scramble eggs and cut up fruit to serve.

Using the eggs from the Easter egg people activity, make a scrambled egg feast to share. Cook the eggs and give each person a small snack of scrambled eggs and pieces of fresh fruit. If there are special Easter food traditions in your congregation, this would be an "egg-cellent" time to share them!

What can we do?

Near the end of the Easter season, on Ascension Day, we hear the command Jesus gave to his disciples to be witnesses to the ends of the earth. How can we obey those words today?

Challenge all participants to dig through their pockets and bags for coins, 50 cents' worth for the 50 days of Easter. Even if we do not travel to the ends of the earth, our offerings can travel there for us. Children can help adults count coins to make 50 cents in any combination of pennies, nickels, dimes, and quarters.

Decide together to which organization or mission of your church your offering will go.

Challenge participants to continue the 50-cent Easter gift every day throughout the rest of the Easter season.

9

Pentecost

for leaders

did you know...?

Pente means "five" and gives this season its name, which in biblical times was the Feast of Weeks, a festival of wheat harvest. It began 50 days after the Passover.

🕯 The Day of Pentecost is seen as the last day of the Easter season, the final day in the "week of weeks," seven weeks of Easter joy and power.

🕯 Pentecost is the third major church festival of the year, following Christmas and Easter.

🕯 Since the Holy Spirit came to all who were gathered with Peter, Pentecost is often called the "birthday of the Christian church," when the good news burned and shone for people of many languages.

🕯 The Pentecost season is the longest of the church year seasons. It can last up to 28 weeks, depending on the date of Easter, and ends on Christ the King Sunday, the Sunday before Advent begins.

look it up

Read the story of the first Pentecost in the Bible in Acts 2:1-47.

symbols of the season

The color for the Day of Pentecost is red, for the fire of the Holy Spirit descending upon the first Christians and also coming to us. The next Sunday, Trinity Sunday, is commemorated with white as a festival Sunday. The rest of the lengthy Pentecost season is represented with the color green to symbolize our ongoing growth in Christ.

Dove The descending dove is often a symbol of the Holy Spirit (see Mark 1:10). Pentecost marks the day when the Spirit presented good news through the disciples as they spoke in various languages. It is that celebration of the Spirit that has made Pentecost a popular day for Affirmation of Baptism, or confirmation, for youth in many congregations.

Flame The Holy Spirit came to the disciples as tongues of fire on the first Pentecost. The movement of a bright flame on a candle reminds us of the motion of the Holy Spirit, at work in our lives constantly.

Wind Although difficult to symbolize visually, the wind is another way to picture the work of the Holy Spirit: sometimes moving quickly, other times gently. Just like the wind, we cannot see the Holy Spirit, but we feel the Spirit's presence and work among us.

Trinity circles Often the symbol of three joined circles is used to symbolize the Trinity—God as Father, Son, and Holy Spirit.

Growing vine The many weeks of the Pentecost season focus on our growth as Christians and also the growth of the Christian church. Any growing plant or vine is symbolic of our deep roots in Christ and the growth that occurs because of the nourishment and support given by the Holy Spirit.

a bulletin board for Pentecost

Materials needed: camera and film, red paper or fabric, scissors, construction paper strips (about 4" x 12") in colors different from the background of the bulletin board.

Pentecost is the time to proclaim "We are the church!" From Acts 2 to the present, church has had more to do with people than with buildings.

Cover a bulletin board with red paper or fabric. Accordion-fold 4" x 12" paper strips and draw a

"We Are the Church!" bulletin board

flame on the top layer that touches both folds. Cut through all layers and use the strip of flames to create a border. Make as many strips as necessary to finish the border around the bulletin board.

Ask church members to help you make living letters to spell your church's name and the phrase, "WE ARE THE CHURCH!" This is a good opportunity to let people of all ages work together in a fun project. Children will learn that they have a big part to play in the project with their great imaginations and agile bodies!

To make the letters, stand together, leaning and bending, to form one letter per photo. For example, to make the letter W: two people sit on the floor facing each other. Place hands under one's knees to help balance and lift feet up in the air to touch the other person's feet to make the center of the W. Take a picture of each group when they perfect their letter.

After the photos are developed, assemble them side by side on the board to spell your church's name under the phrase, "WE ARE THE CHURCH!"

Sunday school opening

Materials needed: red crepe paper streamers; 3" x 8" pieces of white, yellow, or orange construction paper; stapler; scissors.

Preparation: Fold construction paper rectangles in half and cut a flame shape, leaving the fold intact. If students will not be assembling their own Pentecost streamers, follow the steps below and place the completed streamers in the Worship Box. (If you have not made a Worship Box, see page 5 for instructions.) If students will make their streamers, place precut strips of red crepe paper streamers (five or six 18" strips per person) and precut folded paper flames in the Worship Box.

Gather children around the Worship Box and welcome them with an echo prayer, asking children to echo each phrase after you.

Come, Holy Spirit.
Be with us as we worship.
Be with us as we work and play.
May the love of God
burn brightly in our lives.
Amen.

Say: **We prayed that God's love would burn brightly in our lives. Let's figure out what that means. This Bible story will help us:**

Long ago, Peter and some other of Jesus' disciples were together on the day called Pentecost. It was a special day for many people who came to Jerusalem from many different countries. They spoke many different languages.

Suddenly a loud noise like a strong wind began to blow in the place where the disciples were. Then they saw something that looked like tongues of fire come to rest on each person and an amazing thing happened: the disciples were able to speak to all of the people in the city, even those who spoke different languages! God's Holy Spirit was with them to help them do amazing things!

Open the Worship Box and bring out Pentecost streamers. If children are going to make their own,

Pentecost streamer

give simple instructions: Fold the paper flame in half; slip five or six crepe paper strips in the folded flame; and staple through all layers.

Repeat the Bible story, inviting children to wave their streamers as wind and flames are mentioned.

Talk about God's presence with us through the Holy Spirit, then repeat the echo prayer.

activity for young learners

Materials needed: white paper, sand, cake pan, sticks, fish-shaped crackers.

Preparation: Cut the paper into 1½" x 8½" strips. Make one or two strips per child. Fill the pan with a shallow layer of sand.

Jesus' first disciples were fishermen who learned that instead of pulling in their nets of fish, they were called to pull people toward God. At Pentecost, the Holy Spirit gave those disciples power to spread the news about Jesus to even more people by giving them new languages, new words that were understood by all.

Say: **One of the earliest symbols of the church is the fish. It communicated in a nonverbal way during the time when being a Christian was dangerous. As the early church began to grow after Pentecost, a Christian would make half of a fish, one curved line, in the sand or dirt, then wait to see if the other person would complete the fish with a second curved line.**

Explore a variety of simple fish activities as a reminder of the beginnings of the Christian church.

Make paper fish by cutting slits 1" from the ends on opposite sides of the paper. Curve the strip into a fish shape and slip the two slits together. Add a fish face and fins for fun!

Place the pan of sand on a table and let children try in pairs to make the fish symbol just as the early Christians did—one child making a curved line and the other completing the fish.

Enjoy some fish-shaped crackers as a snack together!

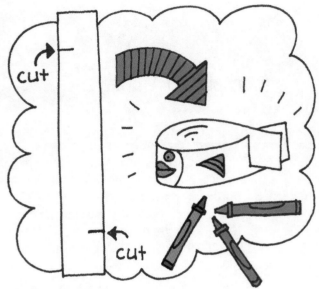

Paper strip fish

activity for middlers

Materials needed: red construction paper; white tempera paint; straws; clear adhesive paper or wide, clear adhesive tape; dove-shaped paper punch (optional).

We are aware of the power of wind and fire in daily life. Talk with students about examples, such as tornadoes, destructive fires, or a controlled fire that can heat an entire home.

Say: **We know what natural fire and wind can do. Imagine how powerful we can be as workers for God if we have God's presence with us as the disciples did at Pentecost. They were able to share God's story with people of many lands. That's powerful! That's awesome!**

Make bookmarks to share with others. As a group, you may decide to make enough to share with another class, homebound members of your church, or even the entire congregation!

On a sheet of red construction paper, place a few large drops of white tempera paint. Now use wind only! Blow through a straw and make designs on the paper by spreading the paint around. Try to make interesting designs on the entire paper.

When the paint has dried, cut the painted sheets into strips 1½" wide and about 6" long. Cut the bottom edge at an angle or with some other decorative cut. Optional: Use a dove-shaped paper punch to make a cutout design on the bookmark strip.

After cutting, cover the bookmark with clear adhesive or tape, leaving a ¼" edge of the adhesive paper or tape around the edge.

all together now
Intergenerational session for Pentecost

welcome!

Materials needed: large sheet of chart paper, markers, scissors.

Preparation: Draw a large outline of your church building or a stylized church building, as a mural. Cut the church into puzzle-shaped pieces, at least 6" in size. Number each piece in the order of assembly of the puzzle, starting with 1 at the bottom and working up. Print "top" on the top of the back of each puzzle piece. If your group is large, you may need to draw more than one church outline to make sure each group gets one puzzle piece.

Gather everyone together and wish them "Happy Birthday!" Sing "Happy Birthday" to the church.

Say: **Today we celebrate Pentecost. Some people call this the birthday of the church because our Bible story for Pentecost tells how the Holy Spirit came to the disciples on that first Pentecost after Jesus ascended into heaven. The Holy Spirit made the disciples able to speak to many people in their own languages, telling them about God's love for us in Jesus Christ. This is marked as the beginning of the Christian church.**

Give each group a puzzle piece and ask them to create a design on the piece to represent how they would describe the Christian church—what the church does, who is a part of the church, what it looks like. Wait to tell participants what their puzzle pieces will form until later.

Instruct groups to check the back side of the puzzle piece and lay their piece with "top" at the top of the back side to make their drawing go the right direction. Use markers to make the pieces colorful. Ask artists to include their names on the front of pieces.

When the puzzle pieces are complete, place them on the floor or a large table. Invite people to put the puzzle pieces together, but don't tell them what the finished product will be. Let them discover it for themselves.

When the puzzle is assembled, tape the pieces together and fasten the puzzle to a wall or large bulletin board.

explore the story

Materials needed: large craft sticks, glue, paper and fabric scraps, camera with instant-developing film, dark-colored blanket or sheet.

Preparation: Ask participants to bring photos of family members to use in this session or bring copies of a church pictorial directory that can be cut up. Have a camera available to take instant-developing pictures of those who may not have photos. Make a Pentecost streamer as described in "Sunday School Opening" on page 45.

Pentecost is a season to celebrate the church, the body of Christ at work in the world. Today's Bible story can be told with puppets, allowing everyone to take part in the action.

Ask everyone to make a self-portrait puppet. Give each person a craft stick. Have each participant cut out and attach the face from a photo of themselves and continue to create the puppet of themselves by adding paper and fabric scraps.

When puppet construction is finished, have a Pentecost puppet show. Bring people up as "puppeteers" in groups. Have volunteers hold the sheet up so that the actors can hide behind it. Ask another person to be the wind and flames of the Holy Spirit and wave the Pentecost streamer behind the puppets at the appropriate time in the story.

Read the story of the first Pentecost, Acts 2:1-21, as the puppeteers act out the story. Repeat the story several times, to let all participate with their puppets.

action for all

Pentecost candles

Materials needed: candle wick (found at craft and variety stores) cut into 5" lengths, paraffin, 3 oz. paper cups, pencils, large measuring cup and pan, red and orange crayons, adhesive tape, vegetable oil cooking spray. This activity requires a kitchen area with a stove.

Pentecost is a time of brightness, the fire of the Holy Spirit, a vivid faith that shows for all to see. Make bright red and orange candles to use at home during the Pentecost season.

Spray the inside of a small paper cup with vegetable oil cooking spray. With a sharp pencil poke a small hole in the bottom of the cup and pull a 5" piece of candle wick up through the hole, bending a 1" piece on the outside of the bottom of the cup.

Wind the loose end of the wick around a pencil resting on the upper rim of the cup. Then place the cup with the wick into another similar sized cup.

Put the paraffin in a measuring cup or small pan that is placed in a larger pan of water at least 2" deep. Have an adult melt the wax over medium high heat on a stove. Add crayon pieces for color.

When the wax has melted, have an adult pour it carefully into the cup with the wick.

The candle will be cool enough to move after a half hour, but wait overnight before tearing off the paper cup. Remove the cups in layers, using a knife if necessary to pare off the layer of wax between the two cups. The base of the inner paper cup could be left on the candle if it's too difficult to remove.

Spirit wind gliders

Materials needed: construction paper, plastic straws, paper, transparent tape.
Preparation: Cut red, orange, or other bright colors of construction paper into 1" x 6" and 1" x 9" strips. Make one glider as a sample.

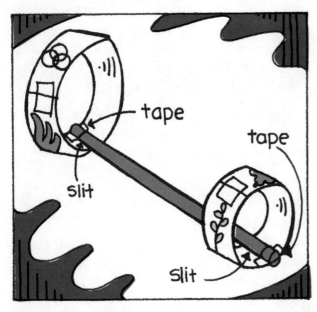

Spirit wind gliders

Experience the wind and remember the power of Pentecost. These spirit wind gliders will fly indoors or outdoors. Imagine the power of the Holy Spirit carrying God's word from one person to the next. The Spirit can come as a gentle, welcome breeze; sometimes it flies like the wind!

Take two strips of construction paper, one 1" x 6" and the other 1" x 9". Decorate as you wish with Pentecost symbols. Tape each strip into a circle.

Cut one slit in each end of a plastic straw. Insert the paper circles into the slits. Secure with tape. Place the small circle at the front and launch your glider!

Growing faith

Materials needed: light green or white construction paper; large seeds such as bean, corn, or sunflower; glue; crayons or markers.

Pentecost is a time for growth. During the season many parables and actions of Jesus' ministry are read. Make a drawing of a faith plant as a collection of ideas for Pentecost growth.

Give each person a seed and a piece of paper. Ask participants to glue the seed onto the paper and draw the growth they think could happen as the seed grows. Some may picture huge vines, others a beautiful flower, others deep roots.

After the plant drawing is complete, ask the participants to write or draw pictures of ways their faith can grow during the long Pentecost season. For example, reading Bible stories after breezy picnic lunches, having worship time under the stars on camping trips, learning a new hymn or song that touches your heart.

Leave time for sharing of ideas as a group.

Encourage them to place their faith plants in a visible spot at home so they can use them as their daily "planters," planting the seeds of faith into their daily "planners" or schedules.

symbols

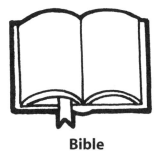
Bible

lamp

manger and crown

baptismal shell

Advent wreath

cross

Christ, the Lamb

trumpets

alpha and omega

angel

Jesse tree

star

globe

chalice and bread

symbols/ID card

palm branches

crown of thorns

three crowns

butterfly

dove

lily

Trinity circles

egg

flame

Child of God

Name _____

Age _____

Hair color _____

Eye color _____

Church's name _____

_____

I'm thumb-body at church!

Luther's seal

Martin Luther created a seal that includes symbols he felt were important understandings about God:

black cross: Jesus' death on the cross for us
red heart: God's great love that gives us life
white rose: trust in Jesus
green leaves: growth in Christ
blue background: a reminder of heaven
gold circle: the never-ending love of God

saint search cards

Directions: Cut on the lines to create Saint Search clue cards. Dates listed on each card are those set aside by many churches each year to commemorate or honor each saint.

Saint Search key: 1. Andrew, 2. Barnabas, 3. Bartholomew, 4. Peter, 5. Paul, 6. James, 7. John, 8. Luke, 9. Mark, 10. Mary, 11. Mary Magdalene, 12. Matthew, 13. Matthias, 14. Michael, 15. Philip, 16. Stephen, 17. Thomas, 18. Nicholas, 19. Martin Luther, 20. Lucia, 21. Martin Luther King Jr., 22. Patrick, 23. Seattle, 24. Francis

1. I was a fisherman, and the first disciple that Jesus called. My brother was Simon Peter. (John 1:35-42) November 30	2. I was an apostle known for being generous, so the other apostles called me "son of encouragement." I was sent to Antioch, then to Tarsus to look for Saul. (Acts 11:19-30) June 11	3. I was called by Philip to follow Jesus. Some people think that my name could have been Nathanael. I have the longest name of all the disciples: 11 letters! (Acts 1:13, John 1:43-51) August 24
4. Jesus called me "the rock" because of my courage and leadership, but there were times I spoke or acted too quickly. But as soon as Jesus called me from my fishing nets, I followed him! (Matthew 16:13-19) June 29	5. I wrote many letters to the Christians in the early church. I traveled with other missionaries—Barnabas and Timothy. My name was Saul until Ananias helped me "see the light" of Christ. (Acts 9:1-19; Acts 13:9) June 29	6. I was a fisherman with Andrew and Peter. With my brother, John, I was sometimes called "a son of thunder" because of my outspoken nature. I was killed because of my faith. (Mark 10:35-45; Acts 12:1-3a) May 1
7. I was a fisherman, a brother of James. One of the gospels in the Bible bears my name. This gospel speaks of Jesus as the light of the world. (Matthew 4:21-22; John 1:1-5) December 27	8. I am credited with writing one of the gospels and the book of Acts. Some think I was a physician. I worked with Paul to spread the news about Jesus to all people. (Luke 1:1-4; 2 Timothy 4:9-11) October 18	9. I am the writer of the Gospel in the Bible that was written earliest, but it is not the first one in the New Testament. Paul and Barnabas sent for me while on their missionary trip. (2 Timothy 4:11) April 25
10. I was Jesus' mother. I am sometimes called the "Christ-bearer" since I brought Jesus into the world. You can bear Jesus' presence into the world, too. (Luke 1:46-55; Luke 2:4-7) August 15	11. I was the first one to tell the disciples about Jesus' resurrection. Don't confuse me with Jesus' mother! (John 20:1-2; 11-18) July 22	12. I left my business as tax collector to follow Jesus. The Gospel that bears my name traces Jesus' family tree back to King David. (Matthew 9:9-13) September 21
13. I am not a well-known disciple. I was chosen to take the place of Judas as one of the 12 disciples. (Acts 1:15-26) February 24	14. I am listed in the book of Daniel as the angel who will lead all to God's throne at the resurrection. I will protect God's children from all forces of evil, including Satan. (Revelation 12:7-12; Daniel 10:10-14) September 29	15. I was called to be a disciple at Bethany. I came from Bethsaida, the city of Andrew and Peter. I was with the other disciples in the Upper Room to meet Jesus after the resurrection. (John 1:43-46) May 1
16. I gave my life as the first Christian martyr. I preached about Jesus and performed miracles, which upset the leaders of my time. (Acts 6:8-15; 7:54-60) December 26	17. I am often called "the Doubter." After the resurrection, Jesus proved to me that he was alive by letting me touch the holes in his hands and feet. (John 20:24-29) December 21	18. I lived in Asia Minor, long after the disciples and apostles of Jesus. When poor people needed money, I secretly gave them some of mine. People still give gifts in my name today at Christmas time. December 6
19. I lived in Germany and began a reform of the church during the 1500s. During my lifetime, I was a teacher, preacher, father, husband, and Bible scholar. One group of Protestant churches bears my name. February 18	20. I was a woman who first helped bring money and food to the poor in my country, Sicily. Then, according to legend, I brought food to people in Sweden who were starving. December 13	21. I lived in the United States from 1929 to 1968. In Georgia where I preached, I created conflicts because of my preaching against discrimination and hatred based on race or skin color. January 15
22. I was born in Britain in the fifth century; later was a slave in Ireland. I escaped after six years. I became a missionary monk and preached, founded churches, and soon became a bishop. March 17	23. I lived in the Pacific Northwest of the United States in the late 1700s until my death in 1866. I encouraged many of my fellow Native Americans in the Christian faith. A city in Washington state is named for me. June 7	24. Although I was born to a rich family, I gave up my wealth to serve the poor. I was concerned about all of God's creatures. I wrote the words for the hymn "All Creatures of Our God and King." October 4

Christr clock

Advent

Christmas

Epiphany

Lent

Easter

Pentecost

(Rally Day)

(All Saints' Day)

(Reformation Day)

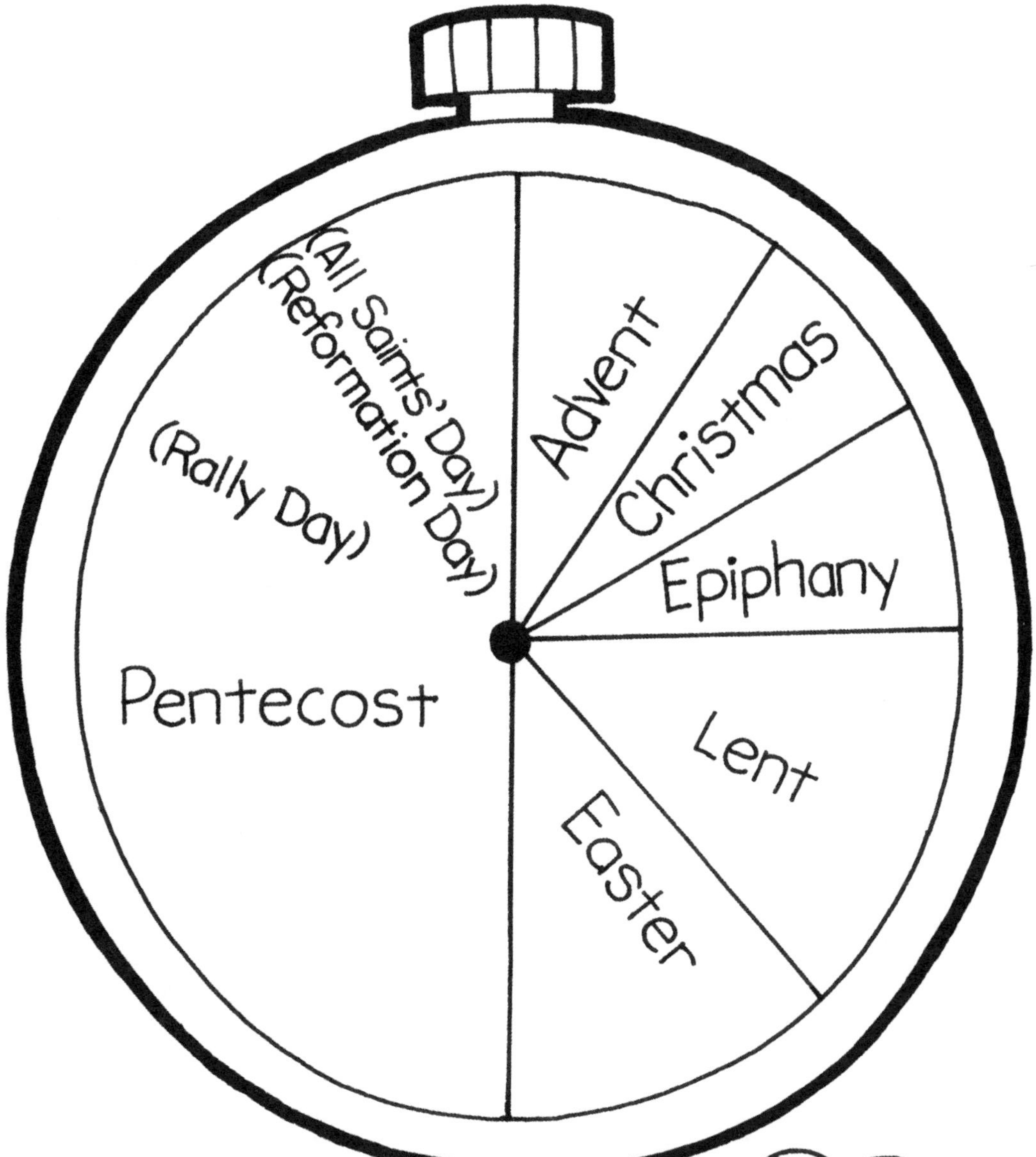

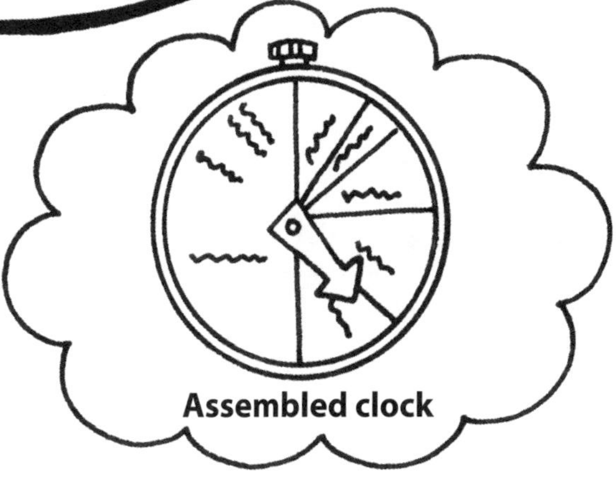

Assembled clock

Nativity figures

you

Lord

is

a

day

To

born

this

the

is

who

Savior

Christ

Epiphany bread recipe

Epiphany Bread

Makes 4-5 small loaves

The quarter hidden in the bread is a reminder of the gifts brought to baby Jesus by the Wise Men. The person who gets the quarter is the "wise person" for the day!

2 tablespoons active dry yeast
1½ cups warm water (105-115 F°)
8 cups all-purpose flour
1 cup sugar
2 teaspoons salt
2 eggs, beaten, and at room temperature
2½ tablespoons butter
½ teaspoon ground cinnamon
¼ teaspoon ground nutmeg
¼ teaspoon ground cloves
1 tablespoon grated orange rind
½ cup orange juice, heated to lukewarm

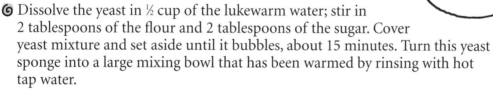

- Dissolve the yeast in ½ cup of the lukewarm water; stir in 2 tablespoons of the flour and 2 tablespoons of the sugar. Cover yeast mixture and set aside until it bubbles, about 15 minutes. Turn this yeast sponge into a large mixing bowl that has been warmed by rinsing with hot tap water.

- Stir into the yeast the remaining water, sugar, salt, beaten eggs, butter, cinnamon, nutmeg, cloves, orange rind, orange juice, and half the flour. Mix with a spoon until smooth.

- Add enough remaining flour to handle easily. Turn onto lightly floured board; knead until smooth, about 5 minutes. Round up the dough in a greased bowl; bring the greased side up. Cover with a cloth. Let rise in a warm place (about 85 F°) until double, about 1½ hours. If the cooking area is cool, place dough on a rack over a bowl of hot water, and cover completely with a towel.

- Punch the dough down. Let it rise again until double. Punch it down and begin shaping into loaves or rounds. While shaping each loaf, place a quarter wrapped in a small piece of foil inside the dough. Finish shaping and place on cookie sheets or in small loaf pans. Let rise until doubled. Bake at 350 F° for 40-45 minutes, or until loaves sound hollow when tapped.

Bible reading strips/ alleluia sign language

Directions: Make a copy of the daily Bible readings for Holy Week for each student to cut out and glue onto a crown of thorns.

Day 1 Matthew 21:1-11	**Day 2** John 12:1-11
Day 3 John 12:20-36	**Day 4** John 13:21-32
Day 5 John 13:1-17, 31b-35	**Day 6** John 18:1--19:42

Sign language for "alleluia"

Clap hands together lightly once.

Then with hands near shoulders, index fingers bent and other fingers in a fist, move hands in circles. The left hand will circle clockwise and the right hand counter-clockwise, both hands circling towards the center of the body.